TRANSMISSION AND TRANSFORMATION:

A JEWISH PERSPECTIVE ON MORAL EDUCATION

Carol K. Ingall
Jewish Theological Seminary of America

Published by the Melton Research Center
of The Jewish Theological Seminary of America
3080 Broadway
New York, NY 10027
(212) 678-8031

MANUFACTURED IN THE UNITED STATES OF AMERICA

ISBN 1-929419-01-5 (soft cover)
ISBN 1-929419-02-3 (hard cover)

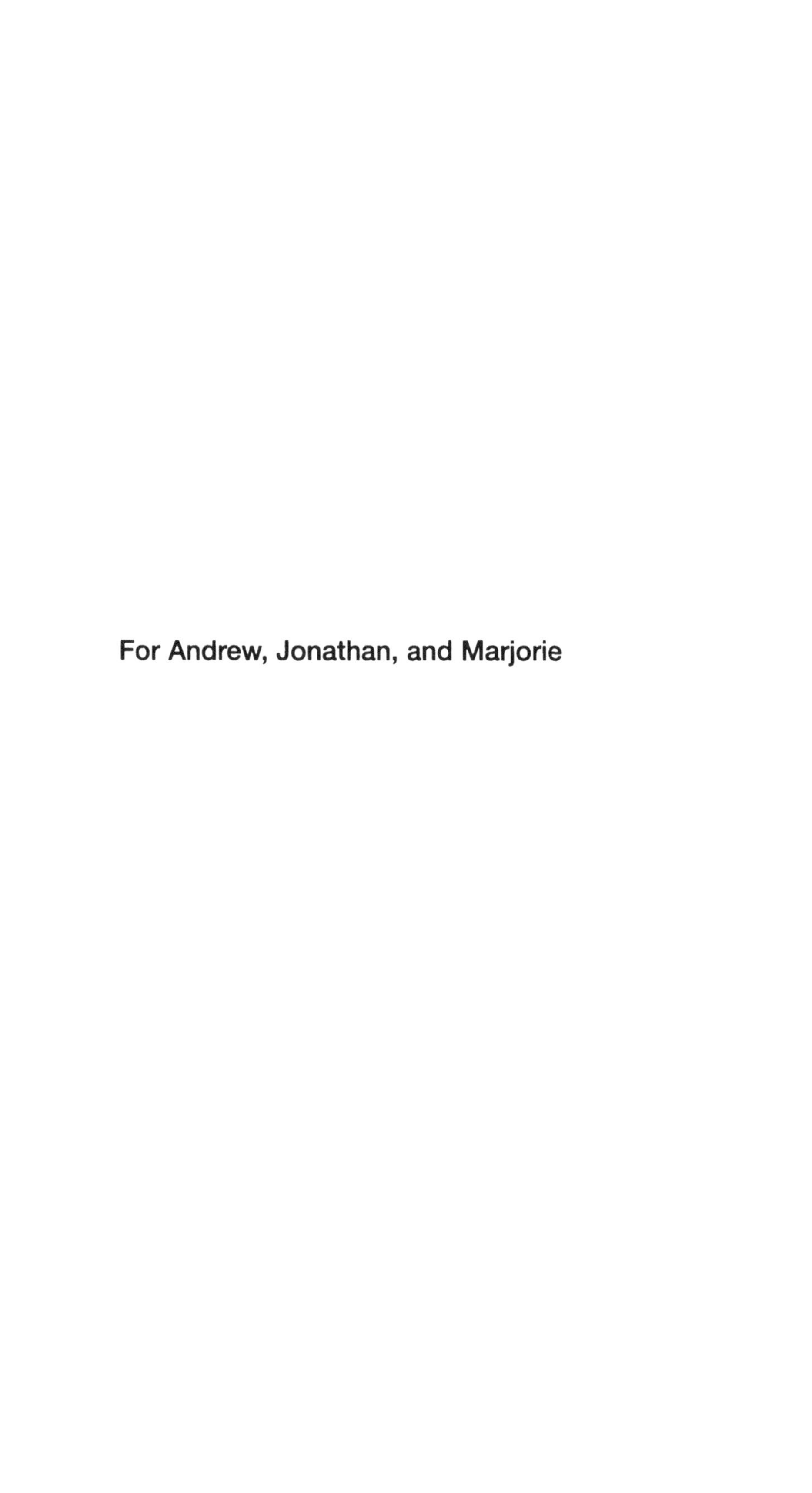

For Andrew, Jonathan, and Marjorie

TABLE OF CONTENTS

FORWARD

It is our delight and pleasure to publish the first in a new series of contributions to the field of Jewish Education called the Melton Library of Jewish Education. Dr. Carol Ingall has set a wonderful framework and tone for a much needed professional literature devoted to pedagogic content knowledge and theories of Jewish educational practice.

While Jews have always borrowed pedagogical and instructional strategies from the surrounding world, we have tried to adapt them to our own particular world view, values, and concentration on the centrality of text as the primary vehicle for conveying our deepest and most profound Jewish sensibilities and understandings of religious practice. In this volume on Jewish moral education Dr. Ingall has combined the best of Jewish thought and experience related to character formation and moral development with an extraordinary practical knowledge of real classrooms, schools, teachers, children, and parents. Thus she has produced an exemplary theory of practice for educational leaders, teachers, researchers, and parents interested in the state and art of Jewish moral education at the turn of the millennium.

The Melton Research Center for Jewish Education is committed to fostering the highest quality research and development of theories of practice and models of curriculum and instruction to help further advance the state of knowledge and the practices of Jewish Education in North America. We congratulate Dr. Carol Ingall on her extraordinary contribution. As you journey through this remarkable work, we trust our readers will enjoy Dr. Ingall's mastery of her subject area, her gifted writing, and deeply sensitive Jewish soul.

Dr. Steven M. Brown
Director
Spring 1999/5759

PREFACE

I am reminded of the speaker who began his lecture with, "Before I begin my remarks, I'd like to say a few words..." This book represents my attempts to respond from a Jewish perspective to the plethora of material on moral education directed to teachers and principals in general education. I say "a Jewish perspective" advisedly. I do not claim to speak for anyone but myself, someone as worried as you readers are about the moral aimlessness which abounds and the paltry attempts of Jewish education to orient its educators and students. I am equally concerned about transplanting the latest fad in general education to Jewish schools, into soil which has a very specific character. Like most moderns, I believe in the isms which make our world different from that which preceded the French Revolution: individualism, rationalism, pluralism, and feminism, to name but a few. Like most of you, I struggle with the tension of accommodating those isms to a traditional Judaism based on holy books which lay out a common past, present, and future for my people, one which emphasizes responsibilities and not rights. One concrete example of my conflict: I struggled with gender-neutral language while writing this book. While I have tried to clean up my language, humility bids me to leave Rashi's, Rambam's, Buber's, and Heschel's alone.

In a world shaped by either/or options, my predilection is for both/and. Not only does that tendency manifest itself in my language, theology, and philosophy, but in my thinking about education as well. I am most comfortable in the borderlands where theory and practice meet. To teach teachers without a connection to the real world of classrooms seems patently fraudulent; to teach teachers as if they were mere technicians denies them their role as professionals. Thus this book plays off that tension as well. Each chapter, from Chapter Three to Chapter 10, begins with theory and ends with practice—a section on school applications I have entitled "Ha-Ma'aseh," "The Practical."

Preface

I have had the opportunity to think through some of the issues that appear in this book while teaching courses in Moral Education at the Jewish Theological Seminary. I am grateful to the Seminary for its grant from the Maxwell Abbell Research Fund for a summer stipend which helped me in doing my research. I am also grateful to my discerning students who have helped to keep me honest. Several of them have contributed to this volume, improving it immeasurably; Jacob Pinnolis, for example, prepared the Hebrew quotations which accompany this volume. I wish to thank Nina Woldin, who lovingly prepared my manuscript for publication. Although I have been enormously enriched by the comments of my generous colleague, Dr. Steven M. Brown, and my beloved teachers, Rabbi Alvan Kaunfer and Dr. Kevin Ryan, as well as the support of my wonderful husband, Michael, the mistakes I have made are my own.

Chapter 1

Establishing the Need

Over one hundred fifty years ago, Søren Kierkegaard, the melancholy Dane, commented on the moral climate of his times in his book, The Present Age. He wrote

> *I once knew a family who owned a grandfather clock whose works for some reason or other had gotten out of order. But the fault did not result in the spring suddenly unwinding, or in the chain breaking, or in the hand ceasing to strike; on the contrary, it went on striking in a curiously abstract, though confusing, way. It did not strike twelve times at twelve o'clock and once at one o'clock, but struck once all through the day at regular intervals. It went on striking all day long but never gave a definite time....* (1940, pp. 19-20)

The calls for moral education are a lot like that grandfather clock--discordant, contradictory sounds, hardly useful as a guide for teaching. Jewish educators are not only being asked to set their watches by that clock, but to repair it as well. Whereas in the past, Jewish schools reflected the moral values of the family and the community, today's schools are supposed to create those values. As one contemporary Jewish sociologist notes, "Jews traditionally educated their children in order to teach them how to live as good Jews. Now parents are urged to enroll their children so that the school may transmit to them the value of being Jewish." (Liebman, 1975, p. 47) Under such circumstances, when the value of being Jewish is not taught at home, it is hardly surprising that Jewish values are not taught at home. Jewish educators have long complained about parental indifference to their educational agendas. Parent-bashing is not unknown in faculty lounges. Yet on the issue of values education, parents welcome a partnership with the schools.

Jewish parents, like their non-Jewish counterparts, are troubled by what they perceive as a moral vacuum in contemporary America. They are concerned about what their children see on television. They are frightened by violence in their schools and streets. They worry about the apparent lack of heroes and role models for their children in a climate which acclaims celebrity instead of courage. Parents who read bedtime stories to their children from Bennett's The Book of Virtues (1993) or Greer and Kohl's A Call to Character (1995) are browsing in bookstores for Jewish equivalents. Some join *havurot*, take adult education courses in the synagogue in order to continue their Jewish education, if theirs was positive, or to redress its failings, if theirs was disappointing. In contemporary parlance, they are seekers after meaning and that search for meaning extends to their children. One of the parents I interviewed mused on her expectations of her children's school: "I was cheated by Hebrew School; I grew up with a post-Sputnik rationality. Other parents are like me, old 60's types. They are searching and longing."

Troubled by the degradation, ugliness, and selfishness in American society, many parents look to the synagogues and Jewish schools to provide their children with the resources to negotiate a terrain filled with moral land mines. The demarcation of public and private spheres that has for so long characterized American religion no longer feels right to them. The nuclear family isn't enough. Like many of their non-Jewish contemporaries, they look to communal institutions to provide them with the resources they need (Bellah et al., 1985; Wuthnow, 1994) These resources are more than Jewish literacy; these parents want moral literacy as well. Teachers cannot get away with being "Jewish information-jockeys"; parents expect them to be moral educators as well. It is striking that in an era when Jewish family education is such a popular buzz-word, when educators so glibly refer to their partnership with parents, that Jewish educators, so ready to teach how to make Shabbat at home, are often reluctant to help parents teach their children to be good.

Our first obligation as Jewish educators is to clarify that just being good isn't enough. Children are already being taught to be good through moral education programs in their public and private schools, in Girl Scouts, and service programs. They collect food for homeless shelters and clean up refuse on Earth Day; they are taught to resolve their conflicts on the playground and to critique their peers' writing with civility. They begin their day with caring circles to share good news and bad. What Jewish educators need to teach them, and what parents may indeed be asking for, is what does Judaism have to teach about being good. What is distinctly Jewish about Jewish moral education? Unless schools and teachers have answered this question for themselves, they can offer little assistance to parents seeking their help.

What is the goal of Jewish moral education? Is it the transmission of time-honored norms in order to preserve a beleaguered Jewish people, beset by defection and intermarriage? Is the goal the creation of a personal values map to find one's way through a shadowy landscape menaced by greed, exploitation, and materialism? It is both, and that is why it is so difficult. Jewish moral education is not a theoretical enterprise, a set of mental exercises devoted to establishing answers to the question, "What is the good life?" That question more accurately belongs to the sphere of ethics or meta-ethics. Jewish moral education deals with the practical. We are first and foremost concerned about behavior. Thus the goal of Jewish moral education must be, in Elliot Dorff's (1995) words, "determining what is the right thing to do in specific settings." (p. 5)

Resistance to the Role of Jewish Moral Educator

Some teachers and principals do not see moral leadership in their job description. Like their colleagues in general education, they play the "not enough time" card. If there is hardly enough space in the curriculum for Bible, rabbinics, synagogue skills, and Jewish history, how can parents ask the teachers to do more? How can beleaguered teachers serve as the agents of a Jewish community hoping to ensure its qualitative as well as quantitative future in a mere four or six hours a week? Is the tight-as-a-drum schedule of a day school any more likely to accommodate a program in moral education? And isn't moral education the parents' job anyway?

My response to them is: ***Like it or not, we are all moral educators.*** Our teaching is laden with moral messages. We communicate these messages in all of our professional interactions: how we greet our students, the seriousness with which we prepare for our classes, the way we treat our colleagues. Through these interactions our students easily decode our moral values: respect for learners ("Cherish the honor of your student as your own" [Avot 4:15], a conscience of craft ("Lazybones, go to the ant; study its ways and learn" [Proverbs 6: 6]), *k'vod habriyot* (honoring God's creation) ("Whoever glorifies himself by humiliating another person, will have no portion in the world to come." [Rambam, Mishneh Torah, Hilkhot Deot 6:3]) As character educator Thomas Lickona declares, "There is no such thing as value-free education." (1992, p. 20) If we are teaching morality anyway, we might as well do so in a reflective, critical, and self-conscious manner. Then too there is the matter of our mission. Whether we teach in day schools or synagogue schools, no matter what the denomination, ours are religious schools. Moral education is at the very core of what we do; echoing the title of David Purpel and Kevin Ryan's book (1976), it comes along with the territory. In Arthur Miller's famous phrase, "Attention must be paid."

A second reason for our foot-dragging is that as goes general education, so goes Jewish education. We Jewish educators have always taken our cues, right or wrong, from secular pedagogy. In the thirties, when American schools experimented with Dewey-inspired, activity-based learning, the "Benderly Boys," the great Jewish progressive educators, began to teach *ivrit b'ivrit*, Hebrew as a language that grew out of the child's experiences. In the sixties and seventies, the Melton Research Center developed curricula for the afternoon school inspired by Schwab's inquiry-based teaching and Bruner's "structure of the disciplines." When the open school swept the American landscape in the seventies, we Jewish educators reconfigured the library as the center of the religious school. With the advent of the eighties and whole language teaching, Jewish schools recast Hebrew instruction in its image. As E. D. Hirsch calls for cultural literacy as a solution to the ills of American public education, there are Jewish educators in the nineties who hope to create a core knowledge program for synagogue schools.

Today general education is awash in moral education curricula with competing claims and contradictory goals. There are programs in promoting student democracy, like Kohlberg's Just Society; values clarification to teach moral reasoning; literature-based character education; self-esteem building; and service learning. Some of our teachers in synagogue schools are teachers in public schools and are adapting general education curricula to Jewish setting without much thought to how well they mesh with Jewish moral values and goals. Others are simply paralyzed by the competing messages they hear: "No hot button issues like abortion and homosexuality." "Teach reasoning not behavior." "Moral education is public health education. We need to teach about smoking, alcoholism, and sexually transmitted diseases."

In the face of such confusion in public schools, it is easiest to shut down and to do business as usual: continue to teach *humash*, Hebrew language, holidays, and skills. In such a climate, moral education is often an afterthought or an add-on. Whether we articulate it or not, we Jewish educators seem to be waiting for our colleagues in general education to figure it out for us. Let them find the magic formula. Once they have discovered what works and taken out the bugs, we will repackage it for Jewish schools, in classically American pragmatic fashion.

But general education is as confused as we are (Remember Kierkegaard's clock), getting mixed messages from its vaunted experts. For example, David Elkind, in The Hurried Child (1988), cautions against too much pressure on a growing child, while William Damon (1995), in Greater Expectations, worries about too little. Lacking a consensus from psychologists concerned with moral development, secular schools duck the big questions and implement piecemeal programs in the name of moral education, such as mandatory school uniforms, multicultural social studies, and naming rules and shaming rule-breakers. We in Jewish education can't wait for general education to get its act together. Our parents want help from us now. David Ackerman's (1997) research on marketing Jewish education suggests that parents are looking to schools to teach Jewish values. It is time to heed Rabbi Tarfon's age-old axiom: "It is not your obligation to complete the task, but neither are you at liberty to desist from it." (Avot 2:20-21)

A third explanation for the inertia regarding moral education in Jewish schools is our unwillingness to come to grips with the "why" of moral education. Some Jewish educators are simply uncomfortable with the philosophical questions the subject of moral education raises. What is the goal of moral education? Is it to inspire awe of the Divine? Social cohesion? A process for negotiating moral dilemmas? Do Jews believe that human beings are innately good or bad? They are unsure of the role of the teacher— an instructor or a facilitator? A tamer of wild beasts or a gardener of beautiful flowers? They may associate the term *moral education* with indoctrination, a word which sets off all their anti-authoritarian alarms.

A fourth source of teacher resistance is closely related to the mission of the moral educator. Many teachers are acutely uncomfortable with the responsibility of being a moral exemplar. Many of them struggle with feeling fraudulent as it is. Staying one chapter ahead of one's students is enervating. (Research on teachers who leave the profession points to fraudulence as a major factor. Anecdotally we all know stories of teachers who burn out because they don't have the resources to draw on.) If teachers worry about not knowing enough, surely they worry about not being "good" enough—having too many lapses in religious and moral behavior. If being a moral educator means being a moral role model—Well, they signed on to teach holidays, period.

A fifth source of resistance comes from those teachers who think they are fulfilling their responsibilities as moral educators, but are not. In this category are the teachers who claim that if they teach their students about ritual observance, they are *yotzei* (they have done what they are duty-bound to do.) These teachers remind me of Michael Rosenak's teacher, who told his charges that unlike a neighboring liberal school, this school did not believe in Jewish values and the students were not going to learn any. "We don't have Jewish values here, boys, we have *mitzvot*." (Rosenak, 1995, p. 147)

Not only does the approach of Rosenak's teacher conjures up a morality which is fixed and frozen, but it can result in bad teaching. The notion that Jewish morality is contiguous with the *mitzvot* lends itself to an older paradigm of education in which teaching is telling and learning is listening. Drill children in *halakhah* and moral education takes care of itself. Such a pedagogy may transmit information, but cannot be considered moral education. It never moves from the realm of heteronomy (reliance on an outside authority) to autonomy (acceptance of the norm after reflection.) Any philosophy of moral education must deal with the triad established by Aristotle and confirmed by generations of philosophers and psychologists: moral education is about knowing the good (learning what the norms are), loving the good (connecting norms to the emotional domain through the imagination), and doing the good (acting in such a way as to comply with the groups norms.) Teaching Jewish values as dusty answers to long-forgotten questions is doomed to failure.

The Focus of this Book: The Eight E's of Moral Education

This book is designed to orient and support the Jewish educator bewildered by the oddly chiming clock of moral education. One way to reset the clock is with a sturdy theoretical framework. (It's a truism that there is nothing so practical as a good theory.) The framework I use was first suggested to me by my mentor, Kevin Ryan, an outstanding moral educator and *mentsch*. Ryan allies himself with the group of moral educators who call themselves "character educators." The term connotes different associations to different people. It can conjure up images of moral indoctrination, Daniel Goleman's emotional intelligence, or Robert Coles's portrait of six-year old Ruby Bridges wading through the waves of white supremacism. I prefer to think of character education in its broadest sense. Remembering Walker Percy's warning about those who get all A's and flunk life, I like to think of character education as making children good as well as smart. (We'll get to the subject of what goodness means for Jewish educators later on.)

I have adapted some of Ryan's views (Ryan, 1988) to reflect my values and my understanding of the field of Jewish education. Where he began with Five E's, I have added three, turning Five E's to Eight. (Inflation is everywhere.) What are the Eight E's? **Excellences, Environment, Experience, Expectations, Explanation, Examination, Exemplars, and Empathy**. I will offer a brief overview of each and elaborate with Jewish sources and curricular suggestions (Ha-Ma'aseh) for implementation in subsequent chapters.

Excellences

Moral education begins with a vision of moral excellences, what philosophers call virtues, and what we Jews call *middot*. What *middot* do we wish to nurture in ourselves and our students? What are the sources of these virtues?

Environment

In traditional circles, one hears the expression, "the walls are *rebbeyim*"—we learn from our environment. The way we treat property and the way we treat people model the *middot* that inform our ethical systems. How do we create in our schools and classrooms the caring environments which make them safe havens in a often uncaring world?

Experience

Traditional Jewish educators believed in the primacy of behavior. Although many of us moderns demand theological support for our practice ("Tell me why, not just how"), we still believe that we should appeal to the young through the experiential. What kinds of experiences can we structure for our students that teach moral education from a truly Jewish perspective?

Expectations

Excelsior—onward and upward. Moral educators are dissatisfied with the status quo. They urge their students to become better people. Classic Jewish texts have filled this function for Jews throughout the ages; for many of us, it was The Little Engine That Could and Aesop's Fables. What role can expectations play in nurturing virtues in a Jewish school?

Explanation

Religious education without explanation is indoctrination. Explanation allows for dialogue, give and take, for questions and answers. By engaging the learner, listening carefully, and providing history and context, explanation saves moral education from becoming an inflexible list of thou shalls or shall nots.

Examination

Examination describes the deliberative process in which the teacher selects the *middot* which undergirds her curriculum. It also describes the process of teaching how to think through a theoretical moral dilemma so that students can practice the skill in preparation for a real-life dilemma. Last, examination is the way students make moral decisions, in their own lives and around issues raised in Jewish texts. Judaism is not interested in automatons, as either teachers or as learners. How do we as Jewish teachers educate for moral autonomy?

Exemplars

One way we learn how to be moral people is through the influence of living models. Like the Hasidim who learned from the way the Tsaddik tied his shoes, children learn from their parents and teachers. They also learn from the heroes of great narratives: from literature, Bible, and Jewish history. How can we harness the power of moral prototypes to foster moral growth?

Empathy

Educators, both teachers and parents, have lately come around to recognizing that the capacity for pro-social behavior and perspective-taking cannot be taken for granted. Although researchers observe that children as young as infants seem to be able to share the pain of others, this proclivity must be developed. To paraphrase Oscar Hammerstein, children still have to be carefully taught. How can we do this in Jewish schools?

The Eight E's have always been a part of Jewish education, although their salience has changed with the time and place. Believing as I do that Jewish moral education, even in the most insulated of settings, is shaped by the trends which mold general education, it makes sense to begin our study with an historical account of moral education in American schools. The historical perspective may not offer any easy solutions to the challenge of teaching Jewish moral values to contemporary American Jews (as I've indicated above, programs in moral education for public and private schools hardly speak in one voice), but by viewing them in context, I hope to offer some insights as to how our Jewish pedagogies and curricula have developed.

CHAPTER 2

MORAL EDUCATION IN AMERICAN SCHOOLS: PICTURES AT AN EXHIBITION

In his important essay, Barry Chazan (1980) distinguishes classical Jewish education from modern Jewish education. Classical Jewish education was collectivist, God-directed, and practical. Its goal was to teach skills and Jewish literacy. By studying God's texts, God's holy people would know what was required of them. Some of these texts, like the Bible and Talmudic literature, were a repository of God's *mitzvot* in both the ritual and moral realm; *mitzvot bein adam la'Makom* (people and God) were intertwined with *mitzvot bein adam l'haveiro* (people to each other.) God commanded, and God's people were expected to obey. Other texts, ethical or philosophical literature, belles-lettres, or hortatory works reinforced the power of authority and demanded compliance through logic, the power of the imagination, or the fear of punishment.

Whereas classical Jewish education sprang from and led to *yirat shamayim* (fear and/or awe of God), the raison d'être of modern Jewish education, in Chazan's view, was group affiliation. The purpose of Jewish education was to socialize young Jews into the Jewish community. Language, liturgy, history, and customs were the mainstays of a curriculum designed to create Jewish identity. Rather than being taught to be a holy people and a kingdom of priests, Jews of the modern era were being taught to belong. By muting the obligatory voice of *mitzvot*, the nexus of religion and morality could be severed. Religious education centered around the stories and symbols of our people, *mitzvot* were good things to do, and moral education was the ethical legacy we Jews gave to the rest of the world.

Nearly twenty years after Chazan wrote his essay, what passes for religious education in Jewish schools is far more complex. Group affiliation is clearly high on the communal agenda as pluralism presents challenges to both the Jewish and general community. But Chazan could not have anticipated the widespread search for personal meaning; his essay, written before Habits of the Heart (Bellah et al., 1985) did not foresee the odd blend of self-realization and communitarianism* which undergirds both religious and general educational life today. He also did not anticipate the search for authority, the post-modern attempts to recreate in some way that older amalgam of religion and morality. Religious education based on behavior and affiliation is not enough. What does it all mean? How can I buy into a system of rules without losing my "me-ness?" How do I reconcile tradition and modernity? The battles over curriculum and canon on college campuses are a reflection of the tumult in Jewish education today. The contemporary challenge to Jewish education as identified by Rosenak (1986), the struggle for authenticity and relevance, is that of general education as well.

To repeat, contemporary American Jewish education is more embedded in general education in America than it is in traditional Jewish sources. Although this is more apparent in liberal Jewish circles, not even the Orthodox camp is immune in an open society. To understand where we as Jews stand in the great values debate sweeping American education, it is helpful to situate the field of moral education in a historical context. I choose to began our amble through American social, intellectual, and educational history with the beginnings of free, public education and the emergence of the common school, from 1830 to the present.

Sociologists of knowledge suggest that ideas are social constructions; these ideas differ from place to place and time to

* "Communitarianism" is a term popularized by sociologist Amitai Etzioni as a reaction to the individualism which characterized much of American behavior in the eighties.

time since they reflect changing societal concerns. School curricula are social constructions. (I use curriculum in its widest sense: all the activities, formal and informal, for which the school is responsible.) Curricula are ideological instruments which reflect and legitimate the institutions that create them: schools, communities, parents, and other authorities. According to the theories of Berger and Luckmann (1966), a curriculum, like any social construction, will act back on its producers; thus knowledge, in our case, moral knowledge, is dialectically connected to social change. As B. F. Skinner (1962) claimed in the gender-specific language of his day, "Men build society, and society builds men." (p. 234) Through their curricula, American public schools transmitted certain values which molded the students who studied those curricula. Students' ideas about the world and their reaction to that world changed them and their children, thus generating new social knowledge and new curricula which would in turn affect the next generation. For example, the conformity encouraged by the schools of the fifties helped to pave the way for the unrest of the Vietnam era; when student protesters advised not to trust anyone over thirty, they were condemning their teachers as well as their parents. The loosening up of language, dress, and sexual mores during the sixties and seventies paved the way for the rampant individualism and materialism of the me-first, yuppified eighties. (I will elaborate on this point later in the chapter.)

How can we study the history of moral education, the changes in what American society values and expects of its children? Just as Mussorgsky created a musical composition based on a stroll through an art exhibit, describing certain paintings which caught his eye, I will review some of the trends in American moral education over the last 150 years through curricular materials and classroom artifacts which symbolize values education at the time, pictures at a moral education exhibition.

The first exhibit is the McGuffey's Third Eclectic Reader, the wildly popular series which sold more than 122,000,000 copies between 1837 and 1920. (Mosier, 1965) This book, designed for third graders, includes stories and questions in the service of building vocabulary and improving reading comprehension. According to the introduction, the goal of the series is to provide a format for "constant drill on good exercises, with frequent exhibitions of the correct method from the teacher." This book, like others in the series, contains snippets of rhyme, Aesop's fables, and legends and lore from world and American history. An example of the material contained in the reader is the poem, "The White Kitten," illustrated with a sketch of a well-dressed young girl, petting a cat sleeping on her lap, posed in front of an open window decorated with house plants. It describes the kitten as having strayed, coming back dirty, "ill-looking" and "beggar-like" and concludes:

> If little good children intend to do right,
> If little white kittens would keep themselves white,
> It is needful that they
> Should this counsel obey,
> And be careful in choosing their places to play.
> (McGuffey, pp. 29-31)

What are the moral messages here? Caution, obedience, and cleanliness are desiderata. White is associated with purity, black with something far less desirable. The young girl's starched pinafore and her carefully pruned house plants have been tended to by those "downstairs" to use the "Upstairs/Downstairs" metaphor popularized by the PBS series. The "hidden curriculum" is much like that of the British scouting movement created by Lord Baden-Powell. Scouting was to be "a character factory," responding to "the need for the lower classes to look to their betters for instruction and moral marching orders." (Rosenthal, 1986, p. 60) So too the common school (the nineteenth century American public school) would be an instrument of social mobility for those children who passed through its portals.

The common school sought to inculcate a middle class, Protestant morality. (It is no coincidence that Catholic Americans began a system of parochial schools at this time.) Curricular materials like McGuffey's Readers relied on the classic techniques of old-fashioned religious education: modeling and moralizing. What counted was how children behaved, not how well they could reason about ethical issues. Virtues (Excellences) like cleanliness, obedience, and caution were identified, preached, and modeled through literary exemplars like the well-dressed girl petting the pristine kitten. Students were expected to come to school with well-pressed clothing and clean fingernails; they were being initiated into the expectations of the larger social order. The school environment reinforced the moral lessons of the teaching materials. Students sat in rows, in front of the teacher's desk; good students turned in neat work, on time, repeating verbatim the material they had been taught.

For our second stop on our stroll, I've chosen a supplement to an American history course designed for eleven- to fifteen-year olds. Blaisdell and Ball's Heroic Deeds of American Sailors was published in 1915, during the heyday of European immigration to the United States. The prevailing form of moral education in American schools during the immigrant era (1895-1935) was what Sidney Yulish (1980) referred to as "civic religion." The role of the teacher was to Americanize immigrant children and their parents. While transmitting the abstract value system of the United States, public school teachers were expected to provide a republican antidote to the radical ideas millions of European immigrants brought along with their samovars, feather pillows, and sepia photographs. Weiss (1982) quotes Ellwood Cubberly, professor of education and former school superintendent, as saying that the task of schools was to "assimilate and amalgamate these people (the immigrants) as a part of our American race, and to implant in their children, so far as can be done, the Anglo-Saxon conception of righteousness, law and order, and popular government." (p. xiii)

The Blaisdell and Ball text is a book of heroes, a panorama of moral Exemplars. These heroes are truly portraits in courage. They include bulwarks of the American republic (still healing from the fissures caused by the Civil War) like Stephen Decatur and James Lawrence, who gave the United States Navy its motto, "Don't give up the ship." Whether on the ocean, on the battlefield, or on the frontier, American heroism was best exemplified by those lonely individuals who lived miles from settled society, but protected it from afar. (American fascination with cowboys, hard-boiled detectives, and more recently, astronauts, are other embodiments of this phenomenon.)

One of the more intriguing heroes included in the book is William Halford, who rescued American merchant seamen stranded on a Pacific island newly captured from Spain. The battlefield is not military, but commercial. Interfering with American trade at the turn of the twentieth century is as threatening a blow to the Republic as was impressing Americans into the British navy prior to the War of 1812.

The strategies of moral education of this era hearkened back to those which preceded them: a delineation of Excellences or virtues that students were supposed to emulate, e.g., heroism and nationalism, and the creation of a moral imagination through symbols and stirring examples. The hero serves to concretize an abstract value or excellence; linked to a thrilling story, the Excellence comes alive to those who hear it. The hero, in the hands of teachers, the agents of society, helps to form ideal citizens, embodiments of civic virtue.

My third exhibit is one of my own souvenirs from public school, a cross-stitched sampler, decorated with bouquets of pink flowers, bearing the epigram "A thing of beauty is a joy forever." I made it for my mother as a Mother's Day present during my mandatory sewing class around 1950. The goal of the Boston public school curriculum was social reproduction: we girls were taught how to be like our mothers (we had classes in sewing and cooking in addition to our academic subjects) while the boys were taught "manual arts," i.e., how to use a hammer and saw like their fathers. The "hidden curriculum," like that manifested in the McGuffey Reader, was uniformity and conformity. The goal of moral education was to initiate the young into society by emphasizing group norms. Textbooks were written on social adjustment, including stories about teens who were ostracized because they didn't shower or use deodorant (Bullis & O'Malley, 1947); handbooks for teachers stressed teaching groups rather than individuals. (Slavson, 1948). Students were introduced to group norms through good citizenship awards, student councils, patriotic assemblies, and of course, teachers who urged them to be good group members, the E of Expectation.

Civic virtue continued to be a concern for moral educators in the public schools. Those of us growing up after World War II studied civics in the ninth grade, American history in the eleventh, and problems of American democracy in the twelfth. Good penmanship was required, along with endless exercises in forming perfect circles and straight lines. In discussing the Palmer Method, one social commentator notes that proper handwriting provided an insight into character. The monotonous drills were necessary in "making intelligent and competent citizens out of the vast body of conglomerate material that comes from Europe." (Rothstein, 7 April, 1997) The E of Experience— drill, practice, and repetition— was an excellent teacher of character.

Little more than ten or fifteen years later, Frederick Wiseman captured the flavor of the relentlessly conformist schools of the era in his cinema verité, High School. One of my favorite moments in the film concerns the young woman who is being lambasted by the principal and guidance counselor for wearing a short dress (instead of the traditional floor- length style) to her prom. They finally bring her to tears; she blurts out by way of apology, "I didn't mean to be an individual." The factory-model high school, designed to label and sort students for college or vocational programs, depended on obedience. The film ends with footage of Vietnam; it is a short hop from high school to the army.

The apathetic fifties gave way to the iconoclastic sixties and seventies. Reliance on Excellences like obedience and nationalism, on Exemplars like national heroes, on Expectations and modeling through Experience, on providing Environments which stressed the transmission of time-honored cultural norms went the way of the "I

Like Ike" button. Rather than emphasizing the group and the needs of society, moral educators sought out techniques and curricula to buttress the individual, to encourage individuation and transformation. The moral education pendulum had swung the other way. For example, the once-prized Palmer penmanship became a relic. Having a unique handwriting became "a proclamation that convention and propriety is for lesser mortals who value appearance over substance." (Rothstein, 7 April 1997, B6)

The types of moral education in the public schools that characterized this period were values clarification and Lawrence Kohlberg's (1969) cognitive developmental model. Values clarification was a reaction to the imposition of values on the young through habit and heroes. Values clarification derided an education based on "the three misleading M's: moralizing, manipulating, and modeling." (Simon & Olds, 1976, p. 18) Responding to a generalized questioning of authority and a fear of indoctrination, teachers at this time emphasized diversity and individuality. In an age of conflicting values, a teacher would best serve moral education by helping his or her students identify their beliefs while sorting through conflicting positions. Values clarification required students to choose the values they espoused, to affirm them publicly, and finally, to act upon them. Proponents of values clarification rejected the moral education of an earlier era as a subjugation of the individual to the collective. Whereas teachers of the older approaches saw themselves as agents of society, committed to creating identity through the inculcation of group norms, the leaders of the values clarification movement imagined themselves as custodians of self-realization. Unlike their predecessors, they were more concerned with the process of moral growth through deliberation rather than the production of good behavior. The operative E's in values education were Examination and Explanation.

One technique of values education ("moral" education with all its normative overtones was eschewed in favor of the less preachy "values" education) was the Values Whip. The teacher, serving as a facilitator of inquiry, would pose a question to the class and provide a few moments for the members to think about their answers. The teacher would "whip" around the room calling upon students to give their answers. Some of the sample questions are: What is something you are proud of? What is some issue about which you have taken a public stand recently? What is something you really believe in strongly? (Simon, Hart, & Kirschenbaum, 1972) Classic values clarification theory included choosing, prizing, and acting; in practice, choosing and prizing were emphasized more than acting on one's beliefs and choices.

Critics of values clarification ranged from old-fashioned character educators who were worried by the implicit "anything goes" in the approach to Lawrence Kohlberg who was equally troubled by its relativism. Drawing on the educational theories of Dewey and Piaget and the moral imperatives of Kantian philosophy, Kohlberg tried to reconnect the moral development of the individual to the background of the social order. Positing that there were six stages of moral development which characterized human growth, Kohlberg delineated a sweeping hierarchy which moved from obedience, to egotism, to the "good-boy" orientation, to duty, to the social contract, and finally, an orientation to individual conscience based on universal principles of justice. Obedience was low on Kohlberg's hierarchy; autonomy, high.

A number of Kohlberg's disciples adapted his theories for classroom use. One such adaptation comes from a slender book of dilemmas entitled Moral Reasoning: A Teaching Handbook for Adapting Kohlberg to the Classroom. (Galbraith & Jones, 1976) One of my favorites, "Sam, the Truck is Here," is designed to supplement a high school American history course. Sam, a former miner, is a grocery store manager in a town in which nearly everyone works in the mines. Planning to strike, the miners try to enlist Sam's support for credit at the store. Sam must choose between loyalty to his friends (who are secretly sending a truck for food) and loyalty to his boss who refuses to allow food to be distributed without payment.

The teacher's role in Kohlbergian moral education was to help her students identify the moral conflicts in the dilemmas and resolve them. By holding up a mirror to the students' moral deliberations, by raising questions in a Socratic dialogue, she would then bring them to a higher level of moral judgment. Kohlberg also recommended that students struggle with real, rather than hypothetical moral dilemmas; he advocated experimental schools ("Just Communities" [Power, 1988]) in which students learned moral education by living it. With the Just Community experiment, Kohlberg wedded the E's of Experience and Environment to the E's of Examination and Explanation.

The eighties witnessed a ferment in moral education. Gilligan and others questioned Kohlberg's hierarchy of excellences, suggesting that the virtue of caring is equally as compelling as that of justice, that being connected is as desirable as being autonomous. (Gilligan, 1982) The feminist assault on Kohlberg's scholarship (he extrapolated his stages of moral development based on male subjects) eroded his credibility and in classic Berger-Luckmann (1966) fashion, the feminist critique acted back on itself. By claiming there was another voice, a feminist morality based on care and responsibility, feminists unwittingly recreated the limiting gender stereotypes from which they had escaped. (Faludi, 1991) With the values clarification movement taking the blame for moral relativism and Kohlberg's cognitive developmental model mortally wounded by the feminist attack, the eighties and nineties engendered a return to older methods of moral education.

The last exhibit on our walk would have to be a collage. Contemporary moral education is a pot-pourri of approaches using literature, heroes, and service projects. Spurred by The Book of Virtues (Bennett, 1993), the runaway best-seller, bookstores teem with anthologies of literature with moral messages. My librarian friends tell me that biographies are once again finding their places on bookshelves and in students' hands. The pantheon of heroes, once the staple of moral education, has been recast. No longer all-white and all-male like those in the Blaisdell and Ball (1915) collection, they include women, minorities, and local heroes. Students are learning about Sacajawea, César Chavez, Amelia Earhart, and Frederick Douglass.

Giraffes in Schools (The Giraffe Project, 1991) is an example of a curriculum which depends on moral exemplars; it asks students to find giraffes, or people who stick their necks out to make their communities more livable. Students are then urged to become giraffes themselves by taking a moral stand on a difficult issuc, by helping others less fortunate than they, or by fighting the new dragons of pollution, urban decay, and indifference.

As community is being rebuilt through heroes old and new, as the more toxic forms of individualism are being countered with new appeals to communitarianism, the E of Empathy, is being addressed in many ways. This collage of moral education in the nineties might include a teacher's handbook on cooperative learning, a flyer announcing that the fifth grade will be visiting their first grade Book Buddies so they can read together, or a photo of an eighth grade working in a food kitchen as part of an on-going service learning project. The E of Experience, habituating children to doing good, whether it is in helping others less fortunate or by learning to stop violence through peaceful conflict-resolution, is once again playing a large role in moral education in today's schools.

As Rashi asked, "*Mah inyan shmitah etzel Har Sinai*?" So what does this have to do with Jewish education? The simple answer is a lot. Each one of these artifacts we encountered during our stroll through American educational history has its Jewish counterparts. My religious school experience during the late forties and early fifties was much like my public school experience; it attempted to socialize me through the acquisition of group values; but rather than emphasizing American heroes and symbols, my Hebrew school taught loyalty to the collective past and to the Zionist future. The American Jewish history books we studied emphasized heroes who moved comfortably in two worlds, like Hayim Solomon,

Mordecai Manuel Noah, Emma Lazarus, and the new breed of hero, the American Zionist, like Mickey Marcus. Affection for the fledgling state of Israel was taught by collecting money for trees on *Tu b'Shevat* and formal assemblies during which "*Hatikvah*" was sung along with the "Star-Spangled Banner". The classrooms of my childhood featured ubiquitous portraits of Theodor Herzl (who conveniently resembled Abraham Lincoln) and colorful posters of kibbutzniks, dancing, picking oranges, or draining the Hula valley. Examples and Environment were the two E's which characterized Jewish moral education during this period.

When moral education in the sixties and seventies in American schools shifted from bolstering the group to bolstering the individual, Jewish education responded in kind. Values clarification found its way into Jewish education. The assumption behind values clarification was that there was no one agreed-upon corpus of moral principles. Personal opinions replaced collective moral authority or divine moral authority. This relaxation of moral obligation was particularly well-suited to informal Jewish education. In camps and youth groups throughout the sixties and seventies, facilitators encouraged the exploration of values around the topics like American-Jewish identity, *aliyah*, the Vietnam War, smoking, drinking, and sex. In his book, Clarifying Jewish Values, Dov Peretz Elkins (1977) discusses the appeal of values clarification for the Jewish educator. He stresses the importance of learning from personal experience; the role of the teacher as facilitator; and the centrality of autonomy. He closes with the following credo:

> *Thus, when I get "preachy" and moralize, and insist that I have the right viewpoint, and the right values, I not only am not an effective educator from a tactical point of view, but I am also shrinking my students' capacity to make judgments and be autonomous, and thus instead of helping them to grow and mature, am keeping them dependent and juvenile. (p. 7)*

Earl Schwartz (1983) was one of many who adapted Kohlberg for Jewish schools. Dismissing moral education based on

Excellences as "a bag of virtues, " Schwartz (p. 9) stresses the importance of cultivating moral judgment through the guided exploration of moral dilemmas. Relying on classical Jewish authorities, he enumerates points of agreement between Maimonides and Kohlberg:

1. Reasoning is an essential part of moral behavior.
2. Human beings pass through stages of moral development.
3. There is a correspondence between age and stage.
4. Moral education must fit the child's stage of cognitive development.

Schwartz accepts the traditional premise that with young children, moral education must begin with extrinsic rewards for appropriate behavior and exposure to powerful role models. With older children, he suggests that teachers should shift to eliciting principled behavior through moral deliberation. (p. 15) His source-book, no longer in print, includes chapters on gossip, reputation, deception, and revenge.

There are Jewish equivalents to all the trends in general moral education: Danny Siegel's (1993) *mitzvah* heroes are Jewish giraffes; Behrman House has a new collection of biographies of diverse Jewish heroes (e. g., Sandy Koufax, Abraham J. Heschel, Steven Spielberg, and Ruth Bader Ginsburg) who exemplify Jewish values (Schwartz, 1996); there are numerous collections of Jewish stories which teach Jewish values (e. g., The ArtScroll *Middos* Books); and *Tikkun olam* projects abound.

Like American public education, Jewish education is torn between transmitting and transforming, between socializing children to group norms and/or encouraging them to question those norms. Transmission is mimetic; it is by its very nature conservative, reproducing the social order as it is or as it was. It is "outside-in" education (Eisner, 1985), in which the teacher, as an agent of the Jewish community, acculturates children into the world of their parents. Some of E's in this book derive from the transmission mode: beginning with absolute Excellences, creating an

Environment to support those Excellences, habituating children through repeated Experiences, and Expecting them to achieve those Excellences. A transmission model of education is concerned primarily with behavior. Transformation is "inside-out" education; children are assumed to have predispositions, opinions, and values which may differ from those of their elders. Those differences must be encouraged, not obliterated. The function of the teacher is to nurture the process of thinking, reasoning in order to make these children autonomous, deliberative adults. Her obligation is not to represent society's interests, but those of her charges. Her task is not to reproduce the social order, but to change it, if it needs changing.

I have depicted some of the significant differences between "outside-in" and "inside-out" moral education below:

MORAL CONCERNS	"OUTSIDE-IN" APPROACH (TRANSMISSION)	"INSIDE-OUT" APPROACH (TRANSFORMATION)
What is more important: Thinking or behavior?	Ethics must precede epistemology: *Na'aseh v'nishma*: proper behavior first, then deliberation	Epistemology must precede ethics: Moral reasoning first, then moral behavior will follow
Which needs take precedence: those of the community or those of the individual?	Society's needs supersede those of the individual. Moral education is for social control and for group cohesion	The individual's needs supersede those of the social order. Moral education is for social reformation and individual fulfillment
What is the nature of the learner?	The learner is at best a *tabula rasa*; a mixture of *yetzer ha-tov* and *yetzer ha-ra*; at worst, a wild creature that requires taming	The learner is innately good and morally capable
What is the role of the parent or educator?	Role of the parent or teacher is to model behavior, to exhort, to admonish, to habituate, and/or to explain	Role of the parent or teacher is to model thinking, to explore jointly with the learner, to facilitate and/or to clarify

The E's of Examination and Explanation clearly belong to the transformative domain. Using Exemplars and teaching for Empathy are techniques which transcend both approaches. The history of the teaching of values in American public schools has been the history of the tensions between "outside-in" and "inside-out" education.

Whether in general education or in Jewish education, I am confident that some balance between the transmission and the transformation modes can be found, that there is a way to be, in Rosenak's phrase, both authentic and relevant. As difficult an endeavor as it is in general education, it is more so in Jewish education. As I write, the loudest voices in the moral education debate (in both general and Jewish education) are those of a neo-conservative timbre. They call for a return to a simpler (and perhaps mythological era) of clear rules, when parents and teachers talked and children and students listened. "Family values" seems to conjure up an Arcadian era when right was right and wrong was wrong, intermarriage was rare, and *mitzvot* were observed. But toothpaste can't be put back in the tube: a need for relevance, reason, and individualism won't disappear. An embattled minority, thriving economically and starving spiritually on the freedom afforded by an open society, may reflexively circle the wagons around the campfire rather than encourage the Examination which characterized the more individually-centered approaches of twenty years ago. The following chapters in this book are an attempt to apply the Eight E's, that balance of transmission and transformation, to moral education in Jewish schools.

Chapter 3

Excellences

As agents of the Jewish community, we educators are entrusted with handing over our cultural and moral heritage to the next generation. We cannot abrogate that authority even as post-modern choruses sing paeans to autonomy, self-fulfillment, and following one's bliss. (We can't ignore them either, but more about that later.) By definition, we teachers are a part of that age-old process depicted in Pirke Avot: "Moses received the Law from Sinai and handed it down to Joshua, and Joshua to the elders, and the elders to the prophets, and the prophets handed it down to the men of the Assembly." (Pirke Avot 1:1) It's humbling to consider, but here we are, past the *geonim* and *aharonim*, the latest links in the chain. How do we know what is essential within the tradition? Having answered that question, how do we then take the raw material and turn it into the stuff of schooling?

I'll begin with the second question and work into the first. As educators we always start at the end. We look at outcomes: what kind of student do we hope to nurture? Or, phrased somewhat more concretely, what kinds of behaviors and attitudes do we want to encourage? One way to conceptualize our task is to define the Excellences we wish to foster in our students. To borrow from the language of character education, what are the moral qualities that make up the essence, the *neshama*, of our students? And now for the second question we Jewish educators need to address: What are the moral qualities (*middot* or *ma'alot*) which our tradition prizes?

Identifying Excellences or as they are more often referred to in the general literature of moral education, virtues, is a standard practice in moral education. In the Nicomachaean Ethics, Aristotle (1985) distills the canon of virtues which made someone an acceptable and admirable member of Hellenistic society, what traits gave him character. Some of the virtues Aristotle includes are bravery, prudence, temperance, generosity, justice, knowledge, fortitude.

and friendship. The Catholic Church derived its cardinal virtues (prudence, justice, fortitude, and temperance) from Aristotle, adding in addition the three supernatural virtues (given by grace) of faith, hope, and charity.

If I were to ask a number of teachers in Jewish schools to define core Jewish values, I imagine that I would receive a diverse number of responses. Justice, for one: "*Tzedek, tzedek tirdof*" Choosing justice as an excellence to strive for leads us in the direction of Kohlberg's "Just Community:" configuring classrooms around the tough decisions thoughtful people need to make in order to provide justice for all. But during the High Holy Days few of us pray for God's justice; most of us are quietly pleading for *rahamim* or mercy. Is this then the central Jewish value? Perhaps, but God showed no mercy to the inhabitants of Sodom and Gomorrah, the gatherer of sticks on Shabbat, or when God refused to heed Moses's pleas to enter the Promised Land.

How about *emet* (truth) as the Jewish Excellence? Truth is surely a strong contender; it was the value which brought life to the Golem of Jewish folklore. According to the Talmud, God's personal seal is truth. But even Aaron the High Priest was said to subvert the truth in order to make peace between warring parties. He is subsequently known as *ohev shalom v'rodef shalom*—one who is a maker of peace and a pursuer of peace. God, according to Baba Mezia 87a, fabricated for the sake of peace, omitting Sarah's characterization of her husband as old when God reported her words to Abraham. We are supposed to be God-like; perhaps *shalom* is the central Jewish value. If we wish to cultivate Jewish Excellence, we should teach texts related to peace and practice peace-making in our classes. However, our tradition has never preached peace at any price. We also believe in the concept of the just war.

In a recent piece, Robert Abramson (1990) stakes his claim for *kedushah* (holiness) as being the Jewish value schools should attempt to cultivate. A truly excellent school would be one which infuses students with awe and wonder, the characteristics identified by Abraham J. Heschel as fundamental to imbuing a sense of the sacred (p. 32)

If we moderns differ on an overriding Jewish value, perhaps there is consensus in the writings of thinkers of the past. In his book of maxims, *Mivhar Ha-peninim* (The Choicest of Pearls), Ibn Gabirol ([11th c.] 1925), the Spanish poet and philosopher, chooses multiple Excellences. He includes on his list of virtues wisdom, patience, faith, fortitude, and contentment, among others. Ibn Gabirol's contemporary, Bachya ibn Pakuda ([11th c.] 1941), delves into the subject of faith and the ethical impulses which should emanate from introspection. He suggests that gratitude for God's goodness would produce the stellar virtue of beneficence to one's fellow beings, a kindness of parents to children, of masters to servants, of the rich to the poor. A century later, another great Sephardic teacher, Maimonides, presents still another view, based on earlier rabbinic sources, on what constitutes Jewish virtue:

> *The sages taught, 'Even as God is called gracious, so you be gracious; even as He is called merciful, so be you merciful; even as He is called holy, so be you holy.' Thus too the prophets described the Almighty by all the various attributes 'long-suffering and abounding in kindness, righteous and upright, perfect, mighty and powerful' and so forth to teach us that these qualities are good and right and that a human being should cultivate them, and thus imitate God, as far as he can. (Twersky, 1972, p. 53—a paraphrase of Sifre Deuteronomy, Ekev)*

In order to cultivate those divine qualities, Maimonides suggests that a student of goodness would do well to examine his or her natural inclinations and try to achieve moderation, Aristotle's middle path.

> *He will not be tight-fisted nor yet a spendthrift, but will bestow charity according to his means and give a suitable loan to whoever needs it. He will be neither frivolous and given to jesting, nor mournful and melancholy, but will rejoice all his days tran-*

quilly and cheerfully. And so will he comport himself with regard to all his other dispositions. This is the way of the wise. Whoever observes in his dispositions the mean is termed wise. (Twersky, p. 52)

In his signature work, *Tahkemoni* (ca. 1220), Judah b. Solomon al-Harizi tries his hand at identifying the core virtues of Judaism. He creates a parable in which seven young men debate about the qualities which God most admires. Humility, promptness, courage, faithfulness, wisdom, culture, and good-heartedness are each nominated as the primary Jewish value. Overhearing their conversation, an old man silences them with testimonials for generosity. (Halper, 1921, pp. 156-161) The 18th century moralist Moses Luzzatto opts for humility (Luzzatto, [1740],1948); the 19th century moralist and father of the Musar movement, Israel Salanter, identifies avoidance of sin and fear of punishment as the wellsprings from which morality flows. In his introduction to Iggereth ha-Musar, Salanter (1858), sounding remarkably like Cotton Mather, to our American ears, answers the age-old question, what qualities lead to goodness:

Man is free in his imagination but bound by his reason. His imagination leads him wildly in the direction of his heart's desire, not fearing the inevitable future, when God will punish him for all his deeds, and he will be chastised by severe punishments, he alone, no other will be substituted for him; he himself will reap the fruit of his iniquities. It will be the very person who commits the sin who will be punished. (Glenn, 1953, p. 128)

From my reading of the sources, there is no consensus on the single overriding Jewish value, the single path to excellence. Choosing one *middah* which epitomizes Jewish teaching appears to be impossible. We have seen that for every virtue we name, there seems to be another which can trump it. In a tradition as values-rich as ours is, we must rely on multiple Excellences. The *siddur*, a primer for moral education, offers a collection of character traits taken from Mishnah Peah 1:1 and Talmud Shabbat 127a that might serve well as core values or Excellences on which to build a Jewish school:

> *These are the things for which no limit is prescribed: the corner of the field (leaving food for the poor), the first-fruits, the pilgrimage offerings, the practice of kindness, and the study of the Torah. These are the things of which a man enjoys the fruits in this world, while the principal remains for him in the hereafter, namely: honoring father and mother, practice of kindness, early attendance at the schoolhouse morning and evening, hospitality to strangers, visiting the sick, dowering the bride, attending the dead to the gave, devotion in prayer, and making peace between fellow men; but the study of the Torah excels them all.*

In looking for Excellences to inform our teaching of morality, we have much to choose from. In the absence of a definitive canon of virtues like that of Aristotle, or the Catholic Church, what yardsticks should we use in choosing Excellences which would both drive our curricula and inform our behavior? For starters, our Excellences have to be framed in Jewish terms rather than universal terms. We as religious educators cannot separate ethics from religion. For a religious person to be good, she has to have a vision of goodness that is rooted in specific religious tradition. (We don't order generic ice cream at Ben & Jerry's; we order specific flavors.) What is our litmus test for Jewish authenticity?

Max Kadushin (1952) introduced the term "value-concepts." Value-concepts characterize what Kadushin called "the rabbinic mind." Not all value-concepts are Excellences; some are core ideas like *yetzer ha-ra*, *nes*, and *malkhut shamayim*. But within the compendium of Jewish value-concepts we can find virtues of a religious-ethical character, moral values which can serve as Excellences.

What are the characteristics of value-concepts? To begin with, value-concepts have the authority of time and tradition. A value-concept is one that has staying power—it is rooted in texts; it has informed Jewish life and practice over time. Kadushin notes that value-concepts, like *derekh eretz* or *tzedakah*, resist translation; in different contexts and over time, they have gained accretions of meaning. Value-concepts are rooted in stories, in the aggadic tradition. The power of the narrative fueled halakhah. "Every rabbinic value-concept had a drive toward actualization" (p. 79) Aggadah made value-concepts come alive in the telling and retelling of stories which created a moral imagination. Halakhah made the value-concept real in day-to-day life. Examples of value-concepts embedded in narrative abound. A few will suffice:

On *Anavah* (Humility)

Our Rabbis have taught: A man should always be gentle as the reed and not unyielding as the cedar. Once R. Eleazar son of R. Shimon was coming from Migdal Gedor, from the house of his teacher, and he was riding leisurely on his donkey, feeling happy and proud of himself because he had studied much Torah. He happened upon an exceedingly ugly man who greeted him, "Peace be upon you, sir." He, however did not return the salutation but instead said to him, "Good for nothing, how ugly you are! Are all your fellow citizens as ugly as you are?" The man replied, "I don't know. But go tell the craftsman who made me, 'How ugly is the vessel that You have made.'"

When R. Eleazar realized he had done wrong, he dismounted from the donkey and prostrated himself before the man and said to him, "I submit myself to you. Forgive me." The man replied, "I will not forgive you until you go to the craftsman who made me and say to Him, 'How ugly is the vessel that You have made.'"

R. Eleazar walked behind him until he reached his native city. When the people of the city came out to meet him (R. Eleazar), greeting him with the words, "Peace be upon you, Teacher, Master," the ugly man asked them, "Whom are you addressing thus?" They replied, "The man who is walking behind you." Thereupon he exclaimed, "If this man is a teacher, may there not be any more like him in Israel." The people asked him, "Why?" He replied, "Such and such a thing has he done to me." They said to him, "Nevertheless forgive him, for he is a man greatly learned in the

Torah." The man replied, "For your sakes will I forgive him, but only on condition that he does not act in the same manner in the future."

Soon thereafter, R. Eleazar, son of R. Shimon, entered the Bet Midrash and expounded, "A person should always be gentle as the reed and let him never be unyielding as the cedar." And for this reason the reed was deemed worthy to be used as a pen for the writing of the Torah, *tefilin*, and *mezzuzot*. (Ta'anit 20a-b)

On *Nekiyut* (Cleanliness)

After Hillel finished a session of study with his pupils, he accompanied them part of the way. They said to him, "Master, where are you going?" "To perform a religious duty," he replied. "Which religious duty?" they asked. "To bathe in the bath-house." "Is that a religious duty?" they wondered. He answered them, "One who is designated to scrape and clean the statues of the king which are set up in theaters and circuses is paid for the work, and he associates it with nobility. Surely must I, who am created in the divine image and likeness, take care of my body!" (Leviticus Rabbah 34:3)

On *Shalom* (Peace-making)

A rabbi was standing in the market-place when Elijah appeared to him. The rabbi asked him, "Is there anybody in this marketplace who will have a share in the life of the world to come?" Elijah answered that there was not. Then two men appeared, and Elijah said, "These two will have a share in the world to come." The rabbi asked them what they had done to earn such distinction. They answered, "We are merrymakers; when we see people troubled in mind, we cheer them, and when we see two men quarreling, we make peace between them." (Ta'anit 22a)

All three of these stories meet the criteria set by Kadushin: set in narrative, value concepts lead to action. This idea is not only a rabbinic one, "*Lo ha'midrash ha'ikar, elah ha'ma'aseh*:" what really counts is the deed, not the discussion), but it is a formulation of virtue well known to Greek philosophy. In his analysis of virtue,

Alasdair MacIntyre (1984) describes moral values as possessing the qualities of practice, behavior, and telos. MacIntyre suggests that a virtue must be rooted in a practice which links the virtue to both the past and the present; the virtue is rooted in a living moral tradition, a set of behaviors. The virtue also requires a telos: a view of what constitutes the good life, a view which the practitioners of that virtue share. These qualities strike me as being useful criteria for identifying Jewish virtues as well.

One Jewish school may feel more comfortable using *tzedek* as the cornerstone of its canon of excellences; another might choose *talmud torah*. The Nahshon School (pseud.) uses *derekh eretz* as an organizing principle which generates a host of caring behaviors. (Ingall, Spring 1998) What seems to me to be essential is grounding those values in Jewish sources and being honest about the lack of unanimity on what constitutes a Jewish Excellence. Just as we must speak of Jewish views (plural) on birth control, euthanasia, and homosexuality, acknowledging that ours is not a monolithic tradition, we must also refer to Jewish views on Jewish virtues.

It's too easy to choose Jewish virtues which fit neatly into the contemporary American zeitgeist. To do so blurs the distinctions between classic Jewish teaching and the American liberal tradition. Fishman (1996) warns American Jews of the dangers of coalescence: dealing with the conflict of living in both American and Jewish worlds by unconsciously merging their world views and moral messages. She is not referring to syncretism, borrowing from a host culture and making it one's own; nor is she referring to synthesis, creating a something new which blends the Jewish and American. What concerns Fishman is more complex: the casual assumption that the Jewish and the American are identical. An example from the realm of values: our concern for ecology. *Bal tashhit* (the rabbinic prohibition against cutting down fruit trees) has become synonymous with ecological awareness and is a cornerstone for moral education curricula in today's Jewish schools. Recycling bins, anti-pollution campaigns, and celebrations of Earth Day are commonplace in religious schools. In fact, *bal tashhit* is not described in 20th or 21st century American environmental terms. In their discussion of why fruit trees could not be cut down in order to build the *Mishkan*, the rabbis link *bal tashhit* , not to the stewardship of the environment, but to *derekh eretz*. This is polite behavior, like the stranger who buys from the local shopkeeper rather than eating food he brings with him. (Shemot Rabbah 35:2) Using a Biblical or rabbinic source for American values is, as Richard Israel asserts, often "a decoration to give apparent substance to values we already have." (Dorff & Newman, 1995, p. 119)

Please don't misunderstand: I worry about the water we drink; I recycle and insist on restaurants providing clean air for diners to breathe. I think all Jewish schools should be careful about wastefulness and want to see recycling bins in the hallways. What I am suggesting is that we do our students and tradition a disservice by wrenching value-concepts out of their rich context and holding out as desiderata only the easy Excellences, those that are most consistent with American values. I would want to couple *bal tashhit* with a more esoteric moral value, one lacking support in American culture, such as *tzniyut* (modesty or appropriateness) or *shmirat ha-lashon* (careful speech.) Such Excellences clarify our distinctiveness and make it clear that Jewish moral education is more than a pareve universalism, that it reflects our distinctive covenant with God.

Firmly believing that schools are rooted in communities and are thus very idiosyncratic institutions, I would not mandate a roster of Excellences for any Jewish school (as long as Kadushin and MacIntyre's guidelines were followed.) Schools have to do this for themselves. Choosing which values to frame the moral vision of a school provides wonderful opportunities for faculties and school boards to study and debate. Having decided upon the Excellences which the school will foster, the stakeholders can move on to implement a program of character education. Besides determining curriculum, these Excellences should frame personnel decisions: Who is an ideal teacher for our school?

First and foremost, Jewish teachers need to embody these

middot. As Heschel suggested, we don't need more textbooks; we need more text-people: men and women who personify the very ideals that are the wellsprings of Jewish morality. As one of the teachers I interviewed mused regarding his commitment to *hakhnassat orhim*, "I'm a little *Avraham avinu*." (Ingall, 1997) In a portrait of Allison Kahn (pseud.), Rhonda Rosenheck (1998) records Kahn's living out (and up to) the value-concept of *talmud torah*:

> *I'm using my intellect an intellect I was given—and I'm using it for the highest purpose for which Jews are given an intellect. I'm studying Torah, which is the highest intellectual and spiritual task given to the Jew. There is an element for me of trying ultimately to go back and to really find out what God wants of us. The only way to do that is by ripping it (a Jewish text) apart and dealing with the* ***Rishonim****, and I really love the process. (p. 12)*

I am enormously concerned about the level of Jewish literacy of our teachers, about their command of pedagogy, and about their mastery of Hebrew. But I am equally concerned about their *mentschlichkeit*, their moral sensitivity. The most important decisions a school can make are personnel decisions. We have seen that aggadah makes an abstraction concrete. So too do teachers who understand that being a teacher means being a moral mentor. (For more on this subject, see chapter 9, Exemplars.

HA-MA'ASEH

1. Many schools, Jewish and general, are creating units on Excellences which cut across the curriculum. Imagine such a unit on *Re'ut* (Friendship) for upper elementary school. It might include Tanakh, the story of David and Jonathan and Job's friends. It could include Mishnah:—Selections from Pirke Avot (2: 9-10), and siddur. (See the personal petitions in the Shaharit service [Siddur Sim Shalom, p.12.] What is a *haver ra*? Can such an oxymoron exist? You might want to add a literature component, like The Secret Grove (Cohen, 1985). Art classes could encourage the design of collages on *Re'ut*, while Hebrew classes would be devoted to the writing of essays on what being a good friend means. (These

cross-curricular units can be designed around other Excellences the school has chosen as central to the school's vision. They afford teachers the all too rare opportunity to plan together how to teach moral education across the curriculum.)

2. Create school and classroom bulletin boards which highlight the Excellences the school has chosen as the curricular foci for the year.

3. Call students' attention to individuals in the news who live lives of Excellence.

4. Capitalize on teachable moments; look for examples of virtues in the curriculum, playground, and classroom. Miriam Zoldan says that in her school, assemblies are held in which children who have done acts of *hesed* are honored: Not by name, nor by identifying the recipients of their kindness, but anonymously, in keeping with yet another Jewish Excellence.

5. Prepare a set of postcards for each child in your class. Pre-address them so they are ready to be mailed home. Look for examples of Excellences in action: kindness, sharing, diligence, perseverance. As you "catch a child being good," send out a postcard to his or her parents. Make sure that each child in the class receives at least one postcard over the year. You know it will be displayed prominently, serving as a reminder to all the family members of the moral dimensions of schooling and the obligation to "train a child in the way he or she should go." (Proverbs 22:6)

6. Dr. Steven Lorch includes examples of student *mentschlichkeit* in his weekly parent bulletin, hoping that these qualities of kindness and concern will be discussed at home as well as in school.

7. Your school library is full of wonderful books which highlight Jewish excellences. One of my favorites is Florence B. Freedman's Brothers: A Hebrew Legend. In this very simple story based on Aggadah, the *middot of gemilut hasadim* (doing acts of loving kindness), *hiddur p'nei zaken* (caring for the elderly), and *kavod av v'eim* (honoring one's parents) are artfully woven.

8. A useful text for high school and adult groups is Judaism and Spiritual Ethics by Goldstein & Mason. It is a selection, in English and Hebrew, of a thirteenth century text by Yehiel ben Yekutiel ben Benyamin Harofe, based on Jewish moral values, called *Sefer Ma'alot Hamidot.*

CHAPTER 4

ENVIRONMENT

A community can further moral sensitivity and moral action or impede it. The stirring saga of Le Chambon, the French village with the remarkable history of saving Jewish lives during the Holocaust, is an example of an environment of goodness (Hallie, 1985); compare that environment with the German ethos depicted by Goldhagen (1996) in his best-seller, Hitler's Willing Executioners. Culture is contextual; morality is situated in community. Pirke Avot 6: 9 epitomizes the rabbinic view on the influence of the setting on an individual's behavior:

R. Yose ben Kisma related: Once I was traveling on a journey. A certain man met me and extended greetings. I greeted him return. He inquired, "From where do you come?" I replied, "I come from a great city of scholars and sages." He said, "Rabbi, if it would please you to live with us in our community, I would give you thousands of gold dinarim, as well as the most precious stones and pearls in the world." I replied, "Though you give me all the silver, gold, precious stones, and pearls in the world, I would not live anywhere except in a community where there is Torah." Moreover, at the time of a person's death, neither silver, gold, precious stones, nor pearls will accompany him, only his Torah and good deeds... (Pirke Avot 6:9, as translated in Siddur Sim Shalom, p. 661)

A rich man tries to lure a great scholar to bring luster to his own community, abundant in resources but impoverished in scholarship. The scholar refuses, preferring Torah to worldly wealth. He cites the Jewish equivalent of "You can't take it with you," and makes the point crucial to this chapter: being in the right kind of community, one predisposed to study, brings longer lasting benefits —protection and guidance in this world and in the next. R. Jose makes the connection between study and good deeds. Living in a community of scholars not only furthers one's scholarship but leads to moral action.

The importance of environment in creating a moral climate is a major leitmotif in the literature of moral education in non-Jewish, as well as Jewish, sources. Aristotle makes the claim that one cannot be moral without a moral community. It is in community that one learns the moral values of justice and friendship; "good people's life together allows the cultivation of virtue." (Aristotle, [4th c.], 1985, p. 259) The father of modern sociology, the nineteenth century Alsatian Jew, Emile Durkheim, is equally insistent on the role of society in fostering human goodness. "If man is to be a moral being, he must be devoted to something other than himself; he must feel at one with a society..." (Durkheim, [1973], p. 79) A theorist of the "outside-in" persuasion, i. e., that morality is taught, not innate, the essentially conservative Durkheim believes that moral norms differ from time to time and place to place (p. 87); since values are embedded in a given community, the family cannot be the sole guarantors of goodness (so much for our contemporary American rallying cry, family values.)

There are a number of studies on how schools shape character by creating environments with clear-cut moral messages. (Rutter et al., 1979; Hill, Foster, & Gendler, 1990; Henry, 1993; Huffman, 1994) Lightfoot's classic, The Good High School (1983) discusses the concept of permeable boundaries and institutional control. Throughout her diverse portraits of "goodness," Lightfoot documents how schools shut out what might be noxious in larger society, creating tight little islands of morality, places with strongly articulated visions of what the good is and how one goes about practicing it. Her school portraits include private and public, suburban and urban, rich and poor institutions, but what they hold in common is a commitment to a vision and what she calls "the societal expectations attached to good mothers: enduring qualities of nurturance, kindness, stimulation and stability." (Lightfoot, p. 311)

Lightfoot's message, and that of today's character educators, is one which fits easily into the world view of Jewish schools. Kevin Ryan, director of Boston University's Center for the

Advancement of Ethics and Character, discusses the creation of a moral environment in language that feels very familiar to Jewish educators. A moral environment is based on religious teachings, surrounds students with ritual and ceremony, has clear-cut rules, generates a vision of the good student, holds teachers to a higher standard, and creates moral literacy. (See the interview with Ryan in Conversations with Educational Leaders [Lockwood, 1997, pp. 13-20.]) Moral education is not confined to a course taught from 9:30-10:15 A.M.; it is not the domain of a specialist, like music or art. It is a school-wide enterprise and as such, depends on the leadership of a principal committed to that enterprise.

To paraphrase the old adage, values (*middot*) are caught as well as taught. In the previous chapter, I presented a case for Excellences. Barbara Gereboff of the Solomon Schechter Day School of Phoenix sent me her general principles for creating an environment which encourages moral as well as intellectual growth. You will note eight of the nine grow organically from value-concepts rooted in Jewish tradition. Each suggests a blueprint for action:

1. We believe that each person is created *B'tzelem Elokim* (in the image of God); therefore, all members of the Schechter community must act with self-respect and with respect for all others.
2. We understand that the Jewish concept of *Rachamim* means that we act with compassion towards all people.
3. *Emet* (honesty) is required to maintain a trusting, viable community.
4. Belief in *Tikun Olam* (making the world better) calls upon each of us to strive for both personal and group success.
5. We believe that we must always be prideful of our identities as contemporary American Jews.
6. Our commitment to *Talmud Torah* (the study of Torah in its broadest sense) demands that we arrive at school prepared and eager to learn and recognize that our education is both an obligation and a privilege.
7. Our belief in *Kavod* (treating people with dignity) and our

efforts to avoid causing *Bushah* (embarrassment) means that we will strive to maintain the emotional and physical safety of all members of our community.

8. Our commitment to *Darkhei Shalom* (pathways to peace) means that we strive to communicate with each other in a peaceful manner.

9. Our understanding of the Jewish concept of *Teshuvah* (repentance) means that we recognize that we all make mistakes, have the capacity to turn away from these mistakes, and are capable of becoming kinder, more caring people.

By sharing its moral excellences with its constituents, a school not only reinforces the moral values of the families it serves, but also sets a framework for communal expectations.

The Role of the Principal

In a discussing school reform, Hill, Foster and Gendler (1990) note that what makes religious schools and magnet schools special is their focus. They have clear missions about academic and moral responsibility. Parents, children, and teachers are expected to abide by social contracts which spell out the formal and informal understandings about the responsibilities of community members. Focus, coupled with religious mission and bounded walls ("What goes on here is different than what goes on outside"), gives Jewish schools enormous latitude in creating moral environments. It is the principal who articulates the mission, who communicates it to teachers, parents, and students, and who realizes it in the environment of her school. (See Sergiovanni, 1992)

The principal's role in promoting moral education, is less a mission and more a vision. She must embody and articulate the Excellences the school has embraced. To reduce her role to keeper of the rules, the umpire who keeps track of "three strikes and you're out" or accountant of the moral trespasses ledger, is no way to create a moral environment. She has to be a visible presence in the school, interacting with faculty, parents, and students.

I have described elsewhere (Ingall, Spring 1998) how one

day school I call the Nahshon School develops a moral climate based upon the ideal of a caring community. The key player in this process is the principal, who has defined her role as instructional leader by infusing her school's curriculum with moral purpose. The process is replicable in both synagogue and day schools. At Nahshon the creation of a caring community is not achieved through a series of commercial curricular or programmatic packages stitched into the fabric of the school. At Nahshon, the curriculum of care is the fabric of the school. Ryan and Cooper define curriculum as "all the organized and intended experiences of the student for which the school accepts responsibility." (1992, p. 266) Thus the curriculum includes the subject matter taught in classrooms, what goes on in the gym, art class, assemblies, and playground. This includes the "hidden curriculum" as well: the messages that are unarticulated but nonetheless pervasive.

At Nahshon, curriculum is created by the faculty, based on Jewish values embedded in Torah or as a response to school concerns. The faculty meets monthly to choose a theme (or Excellence) around which the life of the school will revolve. *B'reishit*, containing the story of Cain and Abel, elicited the theme of "Am I my brother's keeper?;" *Vayera*, including Abraham's encounter with the angel-messengers, evoked the theme of hospitality. These themes provided the structural pegs for both the Judaic and general studies curricula: for classroom discussions, reading, writing, parent involvement, for formal as well as informal activities. Other themes included *bal tashhit* (ecology), respect for the environment, and redemption. The role of the principal is to chair the curricular meetings, to provide the focus, to remind the faculty of their "social contract," and to keep refining the school vision.

The Role of the Teacher

We all know that a school is only as good as its teachers. Although a principal is expected to be a educational leader, her vision is ultimately realized in the classroom. How can a teacher create a moral environment? Lickona (1992) suggests three fundamental conditions:

1. Students should know one another.
2. Students should respect, affirm, and care about each other.
3. Students should feel membership in, and responsibility to, the group. (p. 91)

Thoughtful teachers have developed a repertory of strategies and rituals to achieve these goals. There are classroom meetings, "circle times" devoted to "positive strokes." Once a week a different child is the focus of the meeting; everyone in the class has to say something positive about that child. Other teachers use "circle time" to welcome back children who have been ill or to celebrate special occasions like birthdays and the arrival of new siblings. Some teachers create community through the writing of classroom *b'ritot* (covenants) in which obligations and expectations are defined. (A word of warning: we know from Torah that a *b'rit* must bind both partners. A classroom covenant which deals with the children's obligations and not the teacher's is no *b'rit*. Teachers too have obligations: to treat students kindly, to be punctual, to listen while students speak, etc.) Other teachers pair their classes with older or younger classes as "book buddies" (older students read to younger ones or listen to the younger ones read or practice *tefilot*), to cheer on each other during performances, or exhibitions of mastery (authors' teas, Hanukkah plays, *tzedakah* fairs, etc.)

Lickona's advice on making children feel welcome can be coupled with that of Howard Gardner and his associates. (1983, 1991) In his pioneering work on multiple intelligences, Gardner challenges teachers to be aware of the diversity of talents in the classroom and to highlight intelligences other than the verbal-linguistic and the logical-mathematical. (Most schools place great stock in verbal and mathematical prowess. On the other hand, note what time of day art and music are offered. If there are rooms devoted to these subjects, see where they are located in relation to the layout of the building.) Tapping into musical, artistic (Gardner's spatial intelligence), and physical expression (Gardner's bodily-kinesthetic intelligence) expands the teacher's range of teaching strategies exponentially. The last of Gardner's seven intelligences are the intrapersonal and the interpersonal, what Daniel Goleman (1995) calls "emotional intelligence." The intrapersonal is the ability to know one's self, to find answers to the question, "What does this mean to me?" The intrapersonal includes such domains as can students be reflective about what they learn? Can they apply what they have learned from their lessons to their lives? If our task as Jewish educators is to integrate our students into a world of tradition that is foreign to them, we must afford them the opportunity to make sense of this world. They can do this through journals, through evaluations at the end of units ("What did you like best about our study of Purim?" "What did you like least?") and by working individually on projects that are supervised by the teacher, but chosen by them.

Gardner's seventh intelligence is the interpersonal: the talent of working with others. Working with a study-partner, or *hevruta*, is a time-honored Jewish tradition. In fact, when Joshua ben Perahyah advises us to get a *haver* (Pirke Avot 1:6), he is really reminding us to get someone to study with. *Haver* must be read in context: it directly follows Joshua's suggestion to find a teacher to learn from. One way to incorporate Joshua ben Perahyha's wisdom with that of Howard Gardner is to consider cooperative learning in our schools. (Ingall, 1994) We are taught that *"Ein ha-Torah niknet elah bihavurah"* ("Education is acquired best in groups.") In discussing Pirke Avot 1:6, Jacob Neusner (1984) writes: "Learning is always social, never entirely private. For when we act as if everything depends upon our own judgment alone, we cut ourselves off from criticism. We lose the ideas and stimulation of others. We end up talking to ourselves." (p. 33) As difficult as it is to make cooperative learning effective, it promotes respect for diversity and offers an alternative to the "I swim, you sink" attitude which characterizes much of American education. It also provides an opportunity to break up cliques (even for a short time) and to provide a haven in which quiet children, reluctant to speak before the entire class, can make their contributions.) Most important, for Jewish schools, multiple intelligences build community, a fundamental concern of Jewish life. The wisdom of *"Ein ha-Torah niknet elah bihavurah"* has been embraced by contemporary cognitive psychology.

I am convinced that problem-based learning (Casey & Tucker, October, 1994) in which students and teachers generate questions that truly interest them reap moral as well as academic benefits. The message when learners as well as teachers ask significant questions, and when learners can teach and teachers learn, is a profoundly moral one. It creates an atmosphere of mutual respect; it makes the classroom a learning community in which no one has a lock on expertise. This does not mean we as teachers are absolved of the responsibility for cultural literacy, i.e., transmitting factual knowledge (What are the *shalosh regalim*?) and teaching skills (How to read Torah.) We have the moral responsibility to ensure a Jewish future. But we also have to recognize our students as active learners who have questions about a Jewish present. This too is a moral responsibility.

Our moral responsibilities extend beyond pedagogy to the social and emotional realm. The teacher must ensure a safe and secure environment for each child. A teacher must insist on civility in the classroom. By insisting on civility, the teacher creates a moral environment (civility and civilization come from the same root.) Students can be taught to piggyback their comments on to those of others: "I agree with what Jonathan said because..." or to disagree respectfully: "I disagree with Shoshana because..." Rules need to be balanced with rights. No child has the right to hurt a member of the school community with thoughtless language. Scapegoating, name-calling, teasing, gossip are included under the rubric of *Shmirat ha-lashon*, careful speech and *k'vod habriyot*, paying honor to all of God's creatures. (Needless to say, the rules governing thoughtless speech pertain to teachers and principals. The way we treat our colleagues and support staff, our behavior in the teachers lounge, with parents, and, of course, with our students creates a microcosm of the moral community we wish to build.)

Parents

Creating a moral environment demands the cooperation and support of parents. To do so requires building alliances with them, not as a matter of political expediency, but as partners in the ongoing task of moral education. This means asking them about moral education: what kinds of adults they want their children to become. This means providing them with the know-how they may be searching for: parenting skills, Jewish information, books with moral themes. Parents and school practitioners can work together on broadening their discipline strategies. The current resurgence of rules and codes as a solution to behavior problems (in both homes and schools) is worrisome. Of course, children need to know that acts have consequences. But in order to develop self-discipline, students need to be involved in the making of those rules and their consequences. Parents and teachers can contribute to the building of moral environments by teaching children, even pre-school age, how to handle impulsivity, how to use conflict management, and mediation skills.

Creating a moral environment means recognizing that parents can give as well as receive. A school with a positive moral environment is one in which parents are welcome. To invite them into the classroom to share their expertise is a way of broadening the range of influential adults and authority figures to whom our children are exposed.

Students

Students should be expected to model the excellences which form the moral environment the school espouses. Orientation meetings, school assemblies, student handbooks as well as informal conversations in the hallways between administrators and students and teachers and students serve as opportunities for communicating the moral message of the school. Inviting all the children in the class to a birthday party, picking up papers in the hallways, waiting for one's turn in the school lunchroom are school-wide behaviors which reflect the moral environment of the school. It is disturbing that some of our students define the moral environment of the school narrowly—to the classrooms and hallways. The moral environment of the school must have an elastic dimension which extends it beyond the *dalet amot* (four cubits) of the building—to the playground and bus, for example.

Although public, ceremonial occasions are convenient opportunities to review the kind of environment the school wishes to maintain, the moral environment of a school is best cultivated in classrooms, in the "everydayness" of classroom activities. Classroom discourse should model the excellences fundamental to the creation of an environment of respect and inquiry. One dimension is how students conduct discussions with each other. Magdalene Lampert's (1988) work on the teaching of mathematics is a handbook for creating a moral environment for those who teach Torah. She posits the need to teach students to model intellectual courage (advancing their views although they may not be widely held), intellectual honesty (presenting those views accompanied by evidence), and intellectual restraint (deferring to others in the face of compelling evidence.) She teaches her students to question their peers by saying, "I would like to challenge David's position because...." In such an environment, civility can flourish.

An intensified effort to create a moral environment, both inside and outside the classroom, requires the participation of all the stakeholders of the school. A serious commitment to the enterprise is our only hope of broadening the definition of school environment so that our students begin to understand that whether they are in the building or in the mall, the moral messages of the school aren't left behind when they leave the school grounds.

HA-MA'ASEH

Creating a moral environment in the school:

1. Create school rituals and ceremonies to promote character. Who is your school named for? What elements of good character did he or she embody?
2. Honor students for more than just their academic successes.

3. Post examples of community service on school bulletin boards. Include calls for volunteers, announcements about members of the school community who have been recognized for volunteer service.
4. Use a school assembly to introduce newcomers to the moral vision of the school's founders.
5. Publicly recognize those who work behind the scenes: secretaries, custodians, food service personnel, and parent volunteers.
6. Keep the building spotlessly clean. As one *rosh yeshivah* told me when I commented on how graffiti-free his building was, "The walls are *rebbeyim*."
7. Create study opportunities for teachers to meet with colleagues and study rabbinic texts, literature, or educational research which deals with the issues of moral education.
8. Urge teachers to create an atmosphere in the teachers' lounge that reflects the moral ideals of the school: welcoming newcomers, sharing materials and ideas, refraining from *l'shon ha-ra*, and valuing *talmud torah*.
9. Ask parents to sign up for a goods and services bank. Find ways to use them in the classroom, on class trips, and in school and synagogue projects.

Creating a moral environment in the classroom:

1. Inventory each child about his or her hobbies. Build in an assignment around those interests. A study of Israel could include a component in which each child gets an envelope with an object or artifact that capitalizes on his or her interests. For example, a stamp collector could begin a study of Jewish heroes through a stamp with Golda Meir's picture on it. (The assignments could be individualized or given as group assignments.)
2. Create classroom covenants which bind both students and teachers. Review them through regularly scheduled classroom meetings. Use these meetings to involve students in classroom policy.
3. Do not allow scapegoating, name-calling, or disrespectful language.
4. Be sensitive to gender-related language and activities. Reflect on which children you call upon, discipline, and praise.

5. Overtly teach social skills like good listening and conflict-resolution.
6. Begin the day with a caring circle or brief story from Jewish tradition that deals with Jewish values.
7. Combine healthy doses of support and challenge. Communicate that you care for your students by your concern for them as well as your expectations.

Creating a moral environment in school and at home:

1. Send home information for carpool conversations or Shabbat table talk: Jewish stories, moral lessons from the weekly Torah portion, or new books of interest to parents and children.
2. Create a shared language of moral discourse. The Society for Justice, Ethics, and Morals (Netanya, Israel) generated a list of moral behaviors and their bases in Jewish texts. Both schools and homes could use them effectively:
    a. Smile: "Shammai said, 'Receive all people with a cheerful countenance." (Pirke Avot 1:15)
    b. Greeting: "It is said of Rabban Yohanan ben Zakkai that no one was ever first to greet him, not even a stranger (He greeted everyone before they greeted him.) (Brakhot 17a)
    c. Consideration: "What is hateful to you, do not do unto your colleagues." (Shabbat 31a)
    d. Punctuality: "Beware of stealing someone else's time." (From our sources [sic])
    e. Only one person talks at a time: "Two voices cannot be heard simultaneously." (Rosh Hashanah 27a)
    f. Do not hurt: "One who shames someone else in public is as one who spills blood." (Baba Mezia 58b)
    g. Lower the voice: "The words of the wise are spoken in quiet." (Ecclesiastes 9:16)
    h. Do not gossip (slander): "You shall not go up and down as a talebearer among your people." (Leviticus 19:16)
    i. Put yourself in the other's shoes: "Don't judge your neighbor until you are in his place." (Pirke Avot 2:5)
    j. Do not look at external beauty, but at character: "Look not

at the flask, but at what it contains." (Pirke Avot 4:27); "Who is respected? One who respects others." (Pirke Avot 4:1)

CHAPTER 5

EXPERIENCE

The classical Jewish approach to moral education, of transmitting norms and refining moral behavior, can be found in the response of the Israelites to the revelation at Sinai: *"Na'aseh v'nishma"* ("We will do and we will discern.") Doing the good leads to knowing the good; first the deed (*ha-ma'aseh*), then the deliberation (*ha-midrash*). Like most religiously-based models of moral development, Judaism depends on habituation, the act of repeating experiences in order to educate. In its classical formulation, Jewish religious education maintains that experience is the path to growth—intellectual, spiritual, and moral.

Maimonides underscores the importance of socialization in his Mishneh Torah:

> *How shall a man train himself in these dispositions, so that they become ingrained? Let him practice again and again the actions prompted by those dispositions which are the mean between the extremes, and repeat them continually till they become easy and are no longer irksome to him, and so the corresponding dispositions will become a fixed part of his character." (Twersky, 1972, p. 53)*

Luzzatto too relies on habit as the handmaiden of morality:

> *The habit of humility is acquired through training and reflection. The training consists in gradually habituating oneself to act humbly by always keeping in the background, and by dressing modestly; for a man's dress may be respectable without ostentation. In the way process of becoming habituated to these ways, humility gradually takes possession of a man's heart, until it is firmly established. (Luzzatto, [1948], p. 205)*

Classical Jewish sources expect the parent to be responsible for creating and repeating morally uplifting experiences for his or her child. This pedagogical duty, based on repeated exposure to Jewish experiences, is spelled out in an expansion in Tosefta Hagiga 1:2:

> As soon as children are weaned, they are required to sit in the *sukkah*...When they know how to shake it, they must carry the *lulav*. When they know how to wrap, they must wear *tzitzit*. As soon as they know how to speak, their parents must teach them the *shema*, to read Torah, and to speak Hebrew. If they do not, the children might as well never have come into the world. Children who know how to care for *tefillin* should be given them to carry...(cited by Cooper, 1996, p. 23)

Contemporary parents teach their children in a similar manner. We ask them to say "please" and "thank you" by modeling and by habituation—even before they really understand what the words mean. Eventually those behaviors we deem important are ingrained and integrated into a child's repertoire of responses. These habits, and others like them, not only create a well-mannered child, but they build a moral community, a society which is built on mutuality and civility. We teach *tzedakah* by putting coins into pudgy infant fists and leading them to *tzedakah* boxes; the child delights in finding the opening and hearing as the coins clink. As the child grows older, we augment home activities with those at school, collecting for just causes in North America and in Israel. As theater companies and local symphonies create Young People's Performances in order to build audiences for the future, so too do we Jewish educators (and I include parents as well), rely on early exposure to build life-long patterns.

You recall that Kadushin (1952) posits that an action component is a part of every Jewish value-concept. This action component, or experience, helps to move the Excellence, an abstraction, to the realm of the concrete. Elsewhere I have defined Jewish moral education knowing what is the right (i.e., Jewish) thing to do in specific settings. The operative word here is "do." We begin with the deed. (The absence of the *tzedakah* box or *pushke* in Jewish homes over the last generation made *tzedakah* a matter of writing a check, an activity which hardly invited the participation of children. This critical linkage between a Jewish Excellence and a Jewish Experience was severed. If the recent explosion of lovingly crafted *tzedakah* boxes in gift shops and homes is any indicator, others are equally concerned about repairing this breach between values and practice.)

Contemporary research about the brain and education seems to support what many of us teachers and parents knew intuitively: there is a connection between physical movement and learning. The cerebellum allows for complex decision-making. Peter Strick and his researchers at the Veteran Affairs Medical Center at Syracuse, New York have "traced a pathway from the cerebellum back to parts of the brain involved in memory, attention, and spatial perception. Amazingly, the part of the brain that processes movement is the same part of the brain that's processing learning." (Jensen, 1998, p.84)

It is important to note that neither Torah, nor Luzzatto, nor Maimonides relied on experience alone. The *ma'aseh* was supposed to lead to the *midrash*: behavior alone without discernment was never an ideal. Habit was a prerequisite for autonomy: freely chosen moral decisions and behaviors. Note that repetitive behaviors, not reason, came first. (See Chapters 7 and 8 for a discussion of the *"midrash"* component.) All education, including moral education, must be developmentally appropriate for the learner. What is appropriate for young children is not analysis, but experiences —positive experiences which, as Saul Wachs reminds us, are the stuff from which parents and teachers create Jewish memories. Maimonides describes the process of initiation into learning which infuses an affective dimension to a Jewish experience:

> *Imagine a small child who has been brought to his teacher so that he may be taught the Torah which is his ultimate good because it will bring him to perfection. However, because he is only a child and because his understanding is deficient, he does not grasp the true value of that good, nor does he under-*

> *stand the perfection which he can achieve by means of Torah. Of necessity, therefore, his teacher, who has acquired greater perfection than the child, must bribe him to study by means which the child loves in a childish way. Thus the teacher may say, "Read, (i.e., study) and I will give you some nuts or figs; I will give you a bit of honey." With this stimulation, the child tries to read. He does not work hard for the sake of reading (i.e., studying) itself, since he does not understand its value. He reads in order to obtain the food. Eating these delicacies is far more important to him than reading, a greater good to him. (Twersky, 1972, p. 404)*

Character education in general, whether under Jewish or secular auspices, has acquired an unfortunate reputation for robotic behaviorism. We associate the imitation of sanctioned religious behaviors, including moral behaviors, with compliance, a term that makes us uneasy. Not only do we prefer behaviors that are freely chosen, not routinized, but we're not even certain that habit will produce the patterns we have in mind. Character educators of the nineteenth and early twentieth centuries would choose excellences and then drill their students in the behaviors which exemplified those virtues. In a series of comprehensive studies, researchers Hartshorne and May (1928) found that these behaviors were highly situational. Children refrained from cheating while they were in the classroom with their teachers; however, there was no transfer of training to the world outside the schoolhouse walls. Good behaviors did not become autonomous ones; there was no carryover beyond the classroom when authority figures were no longer present. Sometimes children would cheat and sometimes they wouldn't. (Teachers can attest to the fact that well-behaved youngsters in classroom can become monsters on the schoolbus, playground, or in the lunchroom.) Character education fell out of favor. Forty or so years later, Kohlberg dismissed character education as a "bag of virtues." In its stead, he substituted an approach which began with inquiry in the hopes that action would eventually follow. (He turned *"Na'aseh v'nishma"* on its head.)

Although I deal with the subject of reason in Chapter 8 (Examination), I will offer a preview here: I firmly believe that habituation is not enough. Moral behavior must be coupled with moral process. We are products of Western rationalism; the genies of individualism, pluralism, and choice cannot be shoved back into their lamps. As with any pedagogic venture, moral education demands an array of strategies. A monistic approach is doomed to failure. Moral life is too complex, the process of learning is still too poorly understood, and human beings are far too idiosyncratic to be shaped by habit alone. But to repeat: the starting-point for a moral education rooted in a religious tradition is experience.

This idea is not the preserve of religious educators alone. Emile Durkheim (1858-1917), the father of modern sociology, was one of the first educators to write about the role of habit in moral education. I have chosen to review his work at length because I think it best explains the rationale of the "outside-in," transmission mode of Jewish education, the philosophy behind classical Jewish religious education. Durkheim, like those other intellectual giants, Marx and Freud, had cut his ties to Jewish tradition. However, his views on moral education parallel those of classical Jewish thought. The three elements of the Durkheimian thesis are society, duty, and autonomy. Each is central to Jewish teaching as well. Durkheim, whose father, grandfather and great-grandfather were yeshiva *bochers*, and who himself studied in a yeshiva in Alsace, severed his connection to the Jewish community only after the death of his father and until the lure of the secular world became too powerful to resist (Pickering, 1984, p. 6.) Durkheim reformulated these three concepts, society, duty, and autonomy, secularizing and universalizing some of the principles which had long informed Jewish education.

We have noted that Jewish education in the modern era is about creating group affiliation. We know who we are by forming connections with like individuals. Teachers, who Durkheim compared to secular priests, forge the cohesive bonds of the social order, creating stability for the group and helping individuals to orient themselves. Durkheim claimed that "the domain of the genuinely moral life only begins where the collective life begins--or, in other words, that we are moral beings only to the extent that we are social beings." (Durkheim, 1973, p. 64) People need a community in which to practice being moral. The importance of Durkheim's "collective conscience" is central to Jewish teaching. It is the community, not the individual, which dominates the Jewish world-view. That concern with community can be found in the plethora of self-help organizations that are the hall-marks of modern Jewry. With the arrival of twenty-three Jews to America in 1654 came the pledge that these scruffy refugees would take care of their own. The importance of community also plays out in religious ritual. It is communal prayer that carries the most theological clout, not personal petition. In order for there to be public prayer, there has to be a group of at least ten. Communal prayer is often characterized by recitation in the first person plural. The confessional on the most solemn day of the Jewish calendar, *Yom Kippur*, begins with "We have been guilty"; the credo which epitomizes Jewish faith is "Hear O Israel--the Lord is our God; the Lord is one."

How do we as Jewish educators create a collective conscience? Through initiation. Through the experiential. Through repeated behaviors. We habituate our students to Jewish communal life when we teach prayer, Jewish history, Hebrew language, holiday and daily customs. By participating in Jewish prayer, our students discover the common language and choreography that link Jews horizontally, in Jewish communities across the world. Prayer links Jews past and present in a vertical dimension as well; the *siddur* is Jewry's most beloved book because it has been used for centuries. What Durkheim called social cohesion is a Jewish cultural literacy achieved through repeated behaviors: speaking certain languages, studying privileged texts, doing acts of kindness, celebrating Jewish holidays, and performing the myriad details of Jewish life.

Durkheim's Moral Education is full of references to minorities which draw strength from their marginal status. "With the religious minority, there is a backlog of solidarity, of mutual aid and comfort; there is something unifying, which sustains the faithful against the difficulties of life." (Durkheim, 1973, p. 240) Durkheim's collective conscience, Robert Bellah and Amitai Etzioni's communitarianism, Robert Slavin and the Johnsons' cooperative learning—all recognize the potential of the community to teach, to nourish, and to heal.

A second element in any system of moral education is duty. Durkheim dealt directly with the subject that we Westernized moderns would prefer to avoid. We Americans are very comfortable with the subject of rights; we talk about them all the time. Tolerance is the usual stuff of moral education—respecting the rights of others. When it comes to the subject of responsibility, we liberal Jewish educators become very reticent. The subject of duty, or obligation, makes us profoundly uncomfortable. Durkheim, like the eighteenth century philosopher, Kant, based morality on duty, what we Jewish educators call *hiyuv*, or obligation. "Morality is not, then, simply a system of customary conduct. It is a system of commandments." (Durkheim, 1973, p. 30) To paraphrase the agnostic Jew, Durkheim, we perform moral acts because we are commanded to do so. For Durkheim, it was the state, not religious authority, which commanded its members through its system of laws and customs. Obligation and experience are inextricably linked. "If duty speaks, there is nothing to do but obey." (Durkheim, 1973, p. 31)

It is ironic that Durkheim, the decidedly secular sociologist, had no difficulty with the notion of obligation (what he called heteronomy), and we Jewish educators do. In our discomfort with the notion of obligation, we prefer to discuss *mitzvah* as a good thing to do instead of a commandment. To be fair, the connection of *hiyuv* and goodness is situated in rabbinic commentary. The rabbis noted this dual meaning in their exegesis on the Ten Commandments: "Concerning the large number of ordinances (*mitzvot*), God said, 'I have given you many laws, but also much reward.'" (The Torah, 1981, p. 573) This dual nature of authority, a commanding duty and an inherent good, resurfaces in Durkheim: "Morality appears to us under a double aspect: on the one hand, as imperative law, which demands complete obedience of us; on the other hand, as a splendid ideal, to which we spontaneously aspire." (Durkheim, 1973, p. 96)

The last panel in Durkheim's triptych of moral education is autonomy. For Durkheim, liberty was a by-product of the law. As Everett K. Wilson explains in his introduction to Durkheim's magnum opus, "Only by imposing limits can the child be liberated from the inevitable frustrations of incessant striving." (Durkheim, 1973, xv) This idea is what the philosopher of education, R. S. Peters calls the paradox of moral education: one needs habit—compliance, obedience, heteronomy—in order to become a morally autonomous individual. (Peters, 1981) Durkheim expressed this view by averring that "self-mastery is the first condition of all true power." (Durkheim, 1973, 45) This language is remarkably similar to that of Pirke Avot's "Who is mighty? One who subdues his passions." A famous rabbinic homily on the giving of the law (Exodus 32:16) plays with the interrelationship of liberty and law. "The words were incised, *harut*, on the tablets. One should read *herut*, meaning freedom. The tablets' words spelled freedom for Israel if it would obey them." (The Torah, 1981, p. 652) For Jewish educators to do justice to the conflicting pulls of authenticity and relevance, we must come to terms with heteronomy and autonomy. Downplaying *hiyuv* short-changes the tradition; downplaying the learner's needs, ignores two hundred years of Western individualism.

It is no wonder that the *gemilut hesed* or *tikkun olam* project is one of the mainstays of contemporary Jewish moral education. It is a *mitzvah* rooted in sacred texts and also an opportunity to feel the satisfaction of having done a good deed. It is, in Rosenak's terms, both authentic and relevant. It relies on repeated experiences, establishing the habits through which Jews maintain community. Collecting canned food before *Kol Nidrei* services, ladling stew in soup kitchens, and cleaning up the neighborhood on Earth Day are as much as part of the curriculum of Jewish schools as *Humash*, Hebrew, and *tefilah*. Validated by thoughtful educators like Robert Coles who document the power of "the call of service" (Coles, 1993), Jewish educators in both formal and informal settings use *gemilut hesed* projects to anchor a moral education program. Coles's book is a testament to the power of experience. It is full of examples of young people who began volunteer activities to accompany a parent, to pad a résumé, or to fulfill a requirement. (This is the adolescent, 20th century equivalent of Maimonides' nuts, figs, and bits of honey.) Through their experiences, they found themselves hooked on a life of service, of doing the good. As the rabbis say, *"Mitokh shelo l'shma, ba l'shma;"* what began as a response to extrinsic motivation became intrinsic.

What troubles me about what many schools call *tikkun olam* or *gemilut hasadim* is that what exists is too sparse and too simplistic. Visiting a homeless shelter is a beginning; but one or two excursions cannot possibly create the identification with the other, the role-taking that is so central to pro-social behavior. (Damon, 1990) In fact, the reverse may occur. Ill-conceived programs can engender the arrogance of the *yotzei* (someone who has fulfilled his or her obligation), a sense of hopelessness, or even worse, antipathy. Surely without habituation and study, repeated visits and reflection about those visits, the ideal proffered by Maimonides and Luzzatto will not be reached.

What concerns me more than the programmatic is the ideological. By ideology, I mean the system of representation, through images, myths, and ideas that in unconscious ways, mediate people's understanding of the world. (Althusser, 1976) When what we teach by way of moral education in Jewish schools is identical to the moral mandate of secular schools, then the message we convey is that what Judaism is about, like American civic responsibility, is being a good person. What really counts is being a good person. If one's goodness can be expressed in universal, humanistic terms, then why bother being Jewish? Let me hasten to explain. I want our students to collect clothes for their non-Jewish neighbors who are suffering the ravages of natural disasters. I want them to continue to clean up the neighborhoods in which they live. I would not go so far as Steven Bayme (March, 1996, p. 29), who says that since the Jewish community has embraced *tikkun olam* as its charge, there has been an appreciable increase in assimilation. (This strikes me as *post hoc, ergo propter hoc* reasoning.) What I am asking for is more Jewish substance in service learning—more of that un-American notion of obligation and some distinctively Jewish manifestations of community-building.

We can surely up the ante on our service learning, adding more Jewish sources, and making sure that the experiential is also wedded to the cognitive domain: the *midrash* along with the *ma'aseh*. I want our students to know they are obligated to make the world a better place. But in addition, I suggest that we become more thoughtful about the experiences we choose. I don't want our experiential learning to look identical to those projects done in Boy Scouts or the Lutheran church down the street. To paraphrase Maxine Greene (1985, p. 4), "Surely it is an obligation of [Jewish] education to empower the young to become members of the public, to participate, and play articulate roles in the public space." This means both public spaces which American Jewish youngsters occupy —the Jewish as well as the secular. We paradoxically limit our children's access to public space when we make their experiences too broad. They must be prepared to perform the behaviors demanded by the Jewish community as well.

We can recast our *tikkun olam* projects in more Jewish hues, so that young Jews learn that they have an equal obligation to make the Jewish community more livable and just. There are distinctively Jewish communal experiences that create a moral identity; our children need to be exposed to them as well as the more universal ones. Observing the *mitzvah* of *nihum aveilim* (comforting the mourner) by preparing food for mourners, participating in a *shiva* call, taking turns at attending *minyanim*, provide authentic Jewish experiences which shed light on uniquely Jewish values and initiate young Jews into a very different communal life. Combined with a study of texts, these activities can serve to socialize young people to Jewish norms through Luzzatto's training and reflection, so that they too can affirm *"Na'aseh v'nishma."*

Another approach to service learning is to wed it to problem-solving. In an issue of Phi Delta Kappan devoted to the subject, Kahne and Westheimer (May, 1996) suggest that experience can serve as a springboard for higher cognition. By analyzing a social problem, investigating its origins and manifestations, then strategizing and implementing solutions, students can truly make a difference. I can imagine a group of young people in a camp or community high school learning about *hiddur p'nei zaken* (honoring the elderly) and doing something about the isolation and loneliness of the Jewish aged. Sunday is often the longest day of the week for them. Imagine students analyzing the demographics of the community's Jewish aged, studying nutrition, and the availability of affordable housing. Their research, boosted by the study of Jewish texts and underscored with the concept of *hiyuv* (obligation), could result in political lobbying for low-rent apartments, for friendly visitor programs, for adopt-a-grandparent *shiddukhim* (matches) with local Jewish nursery schools, and for holiday baking.

Cynthia Ozick once referred to the *shofar* with its two openings as a symbol of the Jewish balance of the universal and the particular. Without the two holes, the *shofar* makes no sound at all, let alone rouse young people to assess themselves and their communities. It is time to rethink the experiences we offer our students in the name of moral education lest the sound of the *shofar* be silenced or lost in the din of the trivial and the banal.

HA-MA'ASEH

1. Create a context for Jewish experiences: if you teach prayer, give children an opportunity to pray. If you teach life cycle events, see if your students can be invited as participants in those events (observing a wedding ceremony, a funeral, a *brit* or *simhat bat*.) Inform the parents of your plan; see if they will allow the class to be participant observers.
2. Have children take responsibility for caring for pets and plants, taking them home for *Shabbat* and *hagim*.
3. Create a *bikkur holim* squad: encourage children to call and visit those who are ill, to collect assignments for them, and to provide them with class materials distributed in their absence.
4. Use the rhythms of daily life to teach values-related behaviors: writing thank-you notes in Hebrew, making *shiva* calls, extending

hospitality, welcoming new brides, praying for the recovery of the ill, etc.

5. Use cooperative learning to teach the skills and patience required to work together. There has been an ocean of ink spilled on this subject. You may want to look at my article in The New Jewish Teachers Handbook (Ingall, 1994)

6. Start or expand on a classroom or school recycling project. Ask parents to help you scrounge for items that you can use in your teaching, like fabric remnants, cardboard tubes, plastic containers, and old magazines.

7. Repair worn *siddurim*. Create a *genizah* ceremony in which old books and documents containing God's name are buried. Let our students vividly experience why we are known as "People of the Book."

8. Invite the janitor to the classroom. Have him talk about himself: where he comes from, his family, how long he has been working in the school. Teach the children that they are responsible for the cleanliness of their classroom. Having met the janitor as a visitor, the students are more likely to be more careful about the condition of the classroom.

9. Collect books, toys, and school supplies for some of the new Jewish schools that are being established in Poland, Hungary, Lithuania, and the former Soviet Union.

10. After a unit on rabbinic texts which discuss *tzedakah*, invite a ceramic artist to school to help the children make their own *tzedakah* boxes. With an esthetically compelling ritual object, they are more likely to practice making weekly donations to *tzedakah*.

11. Create a *tzedakah* cooperative. Have the class collect money for worthwhile causes and decide which causes should be the beneficiaries, for how much, and why. Send home directions on instituting a family *tzedakah* cooperative at home as well.

12. My synagogue, Temple Emanu-El in Providence, Rhode Island, invites the entire congregation (all ages) to come to the synagogue kitchen on Christmas day to prepare meals for congregants beset by death or illness. They are wrapped, frozen, and delivered as needed.

13. *Tikkun olam* programs for teenagers must engage them in

meaningful ways. Operation Chicken Soup at the 92nd Street Y in Manhattan does because the teens truly own the program. The participants make their own chicken soup and deliver it to the elderly, people with AIDS, and the homeless. While the soup is cooking they study Jewish sources on hunger and social justice.

11. Some sources:

a. The rabbis taught: "At a time when the people of Israel are in trouble and an individual separates himself from them, the two ministering angels who accompany a person come and place their hands on his head and say: This person who separated himself from the community shall not witness the deliverance of the community." (Ta'anit, 11a)

b. Honi was on a journey and he noticed a man planting a carob tree. He asked him: "How long will it take for this tree to bear fruit? Seventy years, the man replied. Honi then asked him: Are you sure you will be alive in seventy years? The man replied: I found the world ready with previously planted carob trees. As my forefathers planted them for me, I will plant them for my children." (Ta'anit 23a)

c. R. Hama the son of R. Hanina also said: What is meant by the verse: "You shall walk after the Lord your God? (Deut. 13:5)? Is it possible for a mortal to walk after the divine presence? We have been told: "The Lord your God is a devouring fire!" (Deut. 4:24) What it means is that you are to imitate His attributes. He clothes the naked, as it is written: "And the Lord God made for Adam and his wife garments of skin, and He clothed them (Gen. 3:21); you too are to clothe the naked. The Holy One, praised be He, visits the sick, as it is written: And the Lord appeared to him (Abraham, after his circumcision) by the oak of Mamre" (Gen. 18:1); you too are to visit the sick. The Holy One, praised be He, comforts mourners, as it is written: "And after the death of Abraham, God blessed his son Isaac" (Gen. 25:11); you are to comfort mourners. The Holy One, praised be He, buried the dead, as it is written: "And He buried him (Moses) in the valley" (Deut. 24:6); you too are to bury the dead. (Sotah, 14a)

d. Even a poor person who lives on *tzedakah* should practice *tzedakah*. (Gittin, 7a)

e. To minister to the sick is to minister to God. (Abraham Joshua Heschel)

f. The prosperity of a country is in accordance with the treatment of its aged. (Rabbi Nachman of Bratzlav)

g. What is hateful to yourself, do not do to your neighbor. (Shabbat, 31a)

h. Honor your father and your mother just as you honor God, for all three have been partners in your creation. (Zohar, commenting on Kiddushin 30b)

i. Regarding the verse in Exodus 15:2, "This is my God and I will glorify him," the rabbis asked how humans could do justice to God's glory. Abba Shaul responded: "Be like God. Aspire to God's level of mercy and compassion." (Mekhilta d'Rabbi Yishmael)

Chapter 6

Expectations

Both character education and traditional Jewish education have relied on setting Expectations for those they wish to initiate into the community. Educators have been taught to do this from their earliest days of formal training; whether they speak of behavioral objectives, instructional objectives, or learning outcomes, teachers think about standards. (A good deal of contemporary discourse on standards revolves around the question "Do we expect too little of our students?" Heated exchanges on teacher certification also debate the issue of standards, but those standards relate to teachers, not to students.) Such an approach, setting standards and asking the learner to reach them, is a natural for a virtues-based pedagogy. We are concerned as much about outcomes in *mentschlichkeit* as in Hebrew language. Moral education is about norms, and norms require standards. (One definition of norm is a standard.) In order to answer the question "Are we there yet?" we have to know what "there" means.

There is no discussing the "there" without discussing the concept of commandedness. Jewish moral education must meet the question of *hiyuv*, obligation, or Durkheim's duty, head on. We behave in certain ways not only for instrumental reasons—because they make the world a better place to live in or make us feel good—but because we are commanded to do so. How else can we interpret the passage in Deuteronomy which describes the revelation at Sinai?

> *You stand this day, all of you, before the Lord your God—your tribal heads, your elders and your officials, all the men of Israel, your children, your wives, even the stranger within your camp, from woodchopper to waterdrawer—to enter into the covenant of the Lord your God, which the Lord your God is concluding with you this day, with its sanctions; to the end that He may establish you this day as His people*

> *and be your God, as He promised you and as He swore to your fathers, Abraham, Isaac, and Jacob.* ***I make this covenant, with its sanctions, not with you alone, but both with those who are standing here with us this day before the Lord our God and with those who are not with us here this day.*** *(Deut. 29: 9-14)*

Rashi explains that "those who are not with us here this day" cannot mean members of the Israelite nation who were not present. "Moses is not referring to persons who happened to be absent from the assembly, for it states, v. 10, that all were present." Rashi concludes that this phrase is not redundant; the text refers to future generations.

Following Rashi, rabbinic tradition teaches that we too answered, along with the Israelites who heard the commanding voice at Sinai, *"Na'aseh v'nishma"*—that we will obey, we will do God's bidding. The answer indicates recognition of an imperative rooted in the transcendent. *Mitzvot* presume a *Mitzaveh*—a Commander. I acknowledge how difficult this subject is for Jewish educators (myself included.) We are often theologically unsure on this issue: What does believing in God mean? What does obligation (*hiyuv*) mean? We are as uncomfortable with the idea of *hiyuv* as we are with God-talk. We are heirs to the great Western tradition which is based on the rights of the individual. *Mitzvot*, on the other hand, are based on the ultimate "outside-in" model: superimposed by a compelling Deity. Consider the following midrash based on "And they (the Israelites) stood under the mount." (Exodus 19:17) "R. Avdimi bar Hama said: The verse implies that the Holy One overturned the mountain upon them, like an inverted cask, and said to them: If you accept the Torah, it is well; if not, your grave will be right here." (Bialik & Ravnitzky, Eds., 1992, on Shabbat 88a, p.79)

Not an easy passage for an "inside-out" educator who takes the tradition seriously. The late, great French Jewish thinker, Emmanuel Levinas (1994), offers his explanation of the midrash and models a process of reconciling modernity and tradition, authority and reason:

> *Israel is placed below the mountain, if we translate the text literally. The mountain is thus changed into an upside-down bucket. It threatens to crush the tribes of Israel if they refuse the gift of the Law. What wonderful circumstances in which to exercise one's free will—a sword of Damocles!... The teaching, which the Torah is, cannot come to the human being as a result of choice. That which must be received in order to make freedom of choice possible cannot have been chosen, unless after the fact.* (p. *37)*

Levinas refuses to hide from the texts which trouble us moderns. If we are to teach Jewish texts and mores with integrity, we have to acknowledge the "authenticity" side of our "authenticity-relevance" continuum. Authenticity, i.e., faithfulness to the tradition, demands our dealing with obligation, no matter how foreign the concept is to our Western mindset.

Our task is complicated by the fact that contemporary education, particularly in the upper middle class communities in which our students live, is about having a child achieve his or her individual potential. (Research directed at understanding parents' expectations of their children's schools has unearthed a significant socio-economic discrepancy. In more economically privileged families, parents want the school to foster their children's individuality; in lower and lower middle class families, parents want their children to learn the basics, which include obedience.) Traditional Jewish education was "aimed at helping the child to see, accept, and perform the good life rather than to 'realize' or 'express' himself." (Chazan, 1980, p. 304) The good life to which Chazan refers is the life God chooses for us, not the one we choose for ourselves. The reconciliation of these two radically divergent world-views is part of our task as Jewish moral educators.

Authenticity demands that we teach the Excellences which define the norms of the community and expect the members of that community to strive for them. (See Chapter 3.) Elucidating those Excellences and urging the errant or ignorant to achieve them is characteristic of an "outside-in" educational system. According to a transmission model of moral education (and that of religious education which decidedly shares its goals), people are not naturally good; they have to be taught to be good. Jews believe that people have a capacity for good as well as for evil, *yetzer ha-tov* and *yetzer ha-ra*. Maimonides emphatically states the place of free will in educating for moral responsibility:

> *Let it not occur to your mind that God decrees at the birth of a person that he shall be good or evil, a notion expressed by foolish non-Jews and most of the stupid individuals among the Jews. It is not so. Every human being is capable of becoming righteous like Moses or wicked like Jeroboam, wise or foolish, merciful or cruel, niggardly or generous; and so with all other traits. (Maimonides, Mishneh Torah, [1180; 1967], p. 42)*

Moral human beings are not born; they are made. We have seen in Chapter 4 that we teachers make *mentschen* through the Environments we create and in Chapter 5 through the Experiences we frame. Yet another tool is through the Expectations we set. Through Expectations, we set up a moral ideal, raising the bar high enough so that the learner is challenged, but not so high as to make the goal unreachable.

One kind of Expectation that moral educators have used throughout the ages is exhortation—urging the young to improve themselves. Like habituation, the goal of exhortation is internalization. What begins as heteronomous behavior (obedience in order to please an authority) evolves into autonomy (a freely chosen behavior which appeals because of its intrinsic worth.) Exhortation may begin in compliance, but its goal is an appeal to the child's moral imagination. It is a process that turns the thunder and lightening of Mt. Sinai into the still, small voice of conscience.

The Biblical book of Proverbs is a classic example of exhortation, rooted in obligatory behaviors, but designed to reawaken a sense of the Divine Presence, echoes of the mystery of Sinai. Picking verses at random, the reader is aware of the behavioral expectations of the author. "A gentle response allays wrath; a harsh word provokes anger" (15:1) "Do not desert your friend and your father's friend; do not enter your brother's house in your time of misfortune; A close neighbor is better than a distant brother." (27: 10)

Proverbs also identifies the essential moral qualities, Excellences, or *middot* which characterize its "outside-in" approach. The book has a familiar quality for us Westerners, reading like the axioms and aphorisms of The New England Primer ("Pride goeth before a fall") or Benjamin Franklin's Almanac ("A penny saved is a penny earned")—all sources we know better than Proverbs which inspired them! Using adages, warnings, and riddles, Proverbs directs the reader to the aim of Jewish education, his or her telos. That goal is more than just proper behavior, but a life based on the Excellence of *yirat shamayim*, awe of the Creator. Of course, a *yireh shamayim* would behave properly, having accepted what Jewish tradition calls *ol malkhut shamayim* —the yoke of the kingdom of heaven, that is, the performance of *mitzvot*.

Aphorisms and homilies and a concern for proper behavior describe the content of the book. What needs to be added is that Proverbs is also a work of reflection, of deliberation. Like the other wisdom books in the Bible (Ecclesiastes and Job), Proverbs is a self-help book designed to produce a frame of mind, more than just automatic behaviors.

As delineated in Proverbs, the moral process may begin with self-understanding, but self-understanding has its limits. For true insight into ethical behavior, the best source is Torah. Why be good? To demonstrate one's awe of the Creator. One honors through imitation. Why the Torah? To imitate the Creator, the moral individual must reflect upon God's word, God's Torah. Happiness for Proverbs, as for Aristotle, is living the virtuous life. But one arrives at that life only through rigorous study. "Her ways are ways of pleasantness, and all her paths are peace. She is tree of life to them that lay hold upon her, and happy is every one that holds her fast." (Chapter 3: 17-18)

The axioms and exhortations in Proverbs serve as mantras or as the moral equivalents of a string tied around the finger. The purpose of the axioms is to provide the concentration which then leads to action. Moral literature has often served this function. One of my son's favorite books was The Little Engine That Could. It was that book which got him, a cranky nine-year old, up and over the Jerusalem hills during a particularly scorching August. As he strove to keep up with his mother, father, and older sister, I heard him muttering, "I think I can—I think I can—I think I can..." He needed a reminder of the Excellence of perseverance to mobilize him into action, a focusing technique. Watty Piper's classic children's book concretized that virtue. In Jewish sources, concentration is called *kavanah*, a focusing of one's attention.

> *What is meant by the term* ***kavanah****? In its verbal form the original meaning seems to be: to straighten, to place in a straight line, to direct. From this it came to mean to direct the mind, to pay attention, to do a thing with an intention. The noun, kavanah, denotes meaning, purpose, motive, and intention.*
>
> ***Kavanah****, then, includes, first of all, what is commonly call intention, namely the direction of the mind toward the accomplishment of a particular act, the state of being aware of what we are doing, of the task we are engaged in. In this sense, kavanah is the same as attentiveness....*
>
> *To have* ***kavanah*** *means, according to a classical formulation, "to direct the heart to the Father in heaven." The phrasing does not say direct the heart to the "text" or to the "content of the prayer."* ***Kavanah****, then, is more than paying attention to the text of the liturgy or to the performance of the* ***mitsvah****.* ***Kavanah*** *is attentiveness to God. Its purpose is to direct the*

> *heart rather than the tongue or the arms. It is not an act of the mind that serves to guide the external action, but one that has meaning in itself. (Heschel, 1956, pp. 314-15)*

That Jewish focusing to which Heschel refers in prayer can be found in literature as well. Although conventional wisdom characterizes the Talmud as "legal," more than two-thirds of it is aggadic, i. e., folk literature. This literature was recycled in many forms. One was the Ma'aseh Book, a medieval collection of tales which both entertained and educated. Like Aesop's fables or LaFontaine's stories, the Ma'aseh Book used the narrative genre, moral imagination, to urge the reader to higher forms of religious practice. The story of R. Jose's donkey is an example of a fable in which an animal exhibits the kind of behavior God expects of humans:

> *R. Jose had an ass which he let out for hire to those who wanted to ride upon him or to carry burdens, in order to earn some money. And when the ass came home in the evening, he brought the money along, for the people knew the habits of the animal. They tied the money round his neck when he finished his work, and if they put in too much or too little, the ass would not budge, for he was so pious that he would not take more than was due. One day a man hired the animal, hung his pay round his neck as usual, but had forgotten to take off a pair of shoes which were on the animal's back. The ass refused to go home, for he had noticed that there was something hanging from his back which did not belong to him. So he waited till the man took off the shoes, and then he went home. So pious was the ass of R. Jose of Yokreh.* (Gaster, M., (Ed.), [1981], p. 70)

Exhortation communicates to the young the Expectations of their elders. It serves one of the central moral functions delineated by Durkheim: socializing children to the norms of the community. Another genre of Jewish hortatory literature is the ethical will. Judah ibn Tibbon's letter to his son Samuel (Kobler, vol. I, 1978, pp.

156-65) is a well-known example. In it, Tibbon the elder lays out his Expectations for his son, giving us insights as to what the Jews of 12th century Spain and Provence defined as Excellences. Ibn Tibbon's ethical will begins with the value of learning. It includes how Samuel should care for the books in his library; the importance of mastering Arabic, the hallmark of a truly educated man; and the father's insistence that the son study Torah and the science of medicine. Ibn Tibbon also urges his son to work on his handwriting (see Chapter 2 for a reminder of the nexus of penmanship and character), to remember his familial obligations, to be courteous in all his dealings with the public, and to be God-fearing. (Perhaps the ethical will achieved its purpose; the flighty, undisciplined youth to whom it was addressed became a noted scholar, author of a commentary on *Kohelet,* and translator of Maimonides's Guide to the Perplexed.)

The Nahshon School (Ingall, Spring 1998) to which I referred earlier uses exhortation as a means of highlighting moral excellences, producing moral feelings, and inspiring moral behavior. When I visited, I noticed that the school gymnasium was festooned with slogans:

1. Aim for that goal.
2. If it is to be, it is up to me.
3. We will never rest until we make the good better and the better best.
4. Don't be afraid to make mistakes.
5. Sharing and caring
6. Do your best. Never give up.
7. Respect: Give it; get it.

The non-Jewish gym teacher knew that he too was a moral educator. He was quick to tell me that the slogans did not merely serve as moral wallpaper; seizing upon "teachable moments," he would remind his students when they were living up to his Expectations and when they were not.

Rabbi Yitzhak Aboab (Abohav), the fourteenth century Spanish scholar, viewed exhortation as building a bridge between heteronomy (obedience to an outside authority) and autonomy (heeding one's inner voice.) Exhortation coupled with extrinsic rewards leads to proper actions; repetition of those actions, what we have called habituation or Experience in Chapter 5, eventually produces intrinsic motivation. (*Mitokh shelo l'shma, ba l'shma*: Through the deed came the proper intention.)

> *When the child outgrows material rewards, the parent should point out other compensations for learning the Torah. He should tell the child: 'Learn Torah so that you will be seated in the place of honor, you will be called rabbi, and you will be treated with respect.' When this no longer impresses the child, the parents should say: 'Learn Torah so that you will earn a place in the Garden of Eden.' Ultimately, if the child is conditioned to study the Torah, he will come to perceive the truth that lies within it. He will learn to enjoy the study of the Torah. He will develop a love for the Torah and study it for its own sake.* (Abohav, [1984], pp. 38-39)

Exhortation has fallen out of fashion. Its critics seem to feel that within the walls of a school or classroom it is hokey at best, manipulative at its worst. Compare this attitude with what happens on the football field, tennis court, or ice rink. Exhortation rules: coaches, colleagues, and fans create motivation and proper behavior by urging players to remember why they play. Why is exhortation in education passé and exhortation in athletics *de rigeur*? Cheering a team to do its best, encouraging an athlete to hang in even though the odds are against her, applauding examples of grace and courage are all part of the cultural fabric of sports. Coaches are supposed to be exhorters. Why not teachers? One of our tasks as moral educators is to return to the sources, to become coaches of moral actions, thought, and feeling, and to restore exhortation as a legitimate vehicle with which to effect our goals.

Besides exhortation, there are other manifestations of Expectations in our literature. A second is the tradition of self-criticism. The Musar movement, popularized by Rabbi Israel

Salanter in the 19th century, relied heavily on the process of *heshbon ha-nefesh*, or *tikkun ha-middot*, a kind of moral book-keeping that relied on standard-setting and self-evaluation. One approach required students of musar to keep notebooks in which they recorded their daily activities and examined them in the evening. Another, favored by Rabbi Hayim of Volozhin, was a highly individualized, gradual approach. He asked his students to concentrate on self-improvement by working on one area of moral improvement at a time. Yet a third was that of Benjamin Franklin: to list thirteen moral attributes, along with adages and axioms, and to keep track of successes and failures in each of the domains. (Rabbi Menahem Mendel Lefin's [or Levin's] debt to Franklin is well known. The moral attributes Lefin chooses, temperance, silence, order, resolution, frugality, industry, sincerity, justice, moderation, cleanliness, tranquillity, chastity, and humility, are identical to Franklin's. The relationship between Lefin and Rabbi Israel Salanter is not as clear. [Etkes, 1993, pp. 117-134])

A fourth aspect of Expectations lies in the academic domain. For those of us who teach in synagogue or community schools, we have often refrained from making demands on our students or their parents. For example, I suspect that few schools expect regular attendance or are prepared to challenge their students by asking for mastery or for effort. Assigning homework is a rarity. By expecting so little of our students, we damage our image as conscientious professionals. *Hinukh*, education, is a *mitzvah* that requires an attentiveness to the craft of teaching. The Expectations we have for our students are the mirror image of the Expectations we have for ourselves as teachers. Ultimately, we always teach what we are.

In making those demands, we may have to admonish our students, their parents, and colleagues. The Jewish responsibility of *tokhahah*, (rebuke, reproof, or admonition), is one which like *hiyuv*, is at odds with contemporary Western values. Americans revere tolerance; we are all heirs to the "I'm okay, you're okay" tradition. Rebuke is perceived as an infringement of our rights to self-expression. But as Jews, we are commanded to admonish our fellows (Leviticus

19:17-18) if we see wrong-doing. The rabbis inform us that criticism is to be done in private and with the utmost of tact, for "he who puts anyone to shame in public has no share in the world to come." One should never call the backslider by any insulting name, or say anything that would embarrass him or her (Maimonides, *Mishneh Torah*, Deot 6:8.) If we are serious about expectations, how our students and teachers behave in school—how they handle their academic and social responsibilites, then we have to think about using *tokhahah* (admonition) in making us a holier, more moral people.

HA-MA'ASEH

1. Have student select and memorize slogans which express moral attitudes and aspirations. Encourage them discuss why they find them compelling. Decorate the room with these slogans. You may want to turn them into Calderesque mobiles. Find opportunities to weave them into your teaching.
2. If yours is a day school, prepare an integrated unit on fables. Have students create their own fables in Hebrew and English. Perform them for other classes or for visiting parents and grandparents. There are collections of Aesop's fables written with young children in mind.
3. Study selections from Pirke Avot or Proverbs. Have the students create a school mural, mime representations, rap renditions, or their own literary examples to exhort others to moral improvement. Both K'tav and Behrman House have collections on Jewish wisdom literature.
4. You might try to adapt sections of Proverbs for day school use. The admonition of going to the ant to observe her ways is a natural point of departure to study LaFontaine or Aesop's treatment of the grasshopper and the ant.
5. Torah u'Mesorah produces signs based on Jewish exhortations (e.g., "Stop *l'shon ha-ra*" [harmful speech]) which can be used to decorate classrooms and hallways.
6. Discuss the issue of Expectations with the faculty and support staff of the school. Everyone has a role to play in this regard, so include the specialty teachers like art, music, and physical education

staff, custodians, as well as classroom teachers. School secretaries and janitors can expect common courtesy from the student body; teachers and principals can expect that the building be kept clean and graffiti-free. Brainstorm as a group and communicate the results of your discussion with parents and students.

7. Ask students or campers to keep a *heshbon ha-nefesh* (self-evaluation) notebook for a week as some of the musarniks did. Depending on their age and comfort level, they can share their journals with you or keep them for themselves. Ask them to debrief after the process: What did they learn? How did it make them feel? Was there any value in the process?

8. Create a curricular unit on ethical wills. Have the students write wills for their children communicating their expectations. You might want to consult Israel Abrahams's classic work (1926) and Riemer and Stampfer's (1983) more contemporary one for background.

9. With high school students, compare Polonius's remarks to Laertes in Hamlet with Judah Ibn Tibbon's letter to his son (Kobler, 1978). Have them follow up by writing ethical wills for famous fathers to their children.

10. Renée Ghert-Zand, Director of Judaic Studies of the Solomon Schechter High School of New York and I are creating an integrated curriculum for Jewish history and American history comparing the moral education of Benjamin Franklin delineated in his Autobiography with that of Rabbi Israel Salanter and his disciples. Each depended on an identification of central principles of behavior, keeping journals to account for one's conduct concerning that principle, and reciting and memorizing aphorisms to concentrate on those behaviors.

11. Start an ethical will project with the parents in your school. It might begin by asking parents to study Jewish ethical wills (see the sources listed above) and write their own for their children. Temple Emanu-El in Providence printed up such a booklet and made it available to the membership in hopes of inspiring others to try their hand at creating ethical wills.

12. Yet another family education program, with thanks to Aviva Weintraub and Andrew Ingall of the Jewish Museum's National Jewish Archive of Broadcasting: Have families view together and

discuss a television program that deals with Expectations. Aviva and Andrew collected clips from television programs dealing with Bar and Bat Mitzvah. You might want to use a segment on adolescent behavior, relationships between siblings, or parents and children as a springboard for a discussion of television as a compelling arbiter of expectations. Depending upon the group, you may want to couple the discussion with Jewish texts on similar subjects (e.g., *hiddur p'nei zaken* [dealing with the elderly], *kibbud av v'elm* [honoring one's parents], and rabbinic Expectations of parents to their children.)

13. Expectations pertain to parents as well as students. Make sure parents know what the proper procedure is for registering a complaint about a school issue. Inform them that there are Expectations that a classroom issue should be first raised with the teacher involved, before taking it to a parents' association, the principal and the court of popular opinion, the supermarket.

Chapter 7

Explanation

The "outside-in," transmission style of educating the young has gotten bad press since the sixties and seventies. During that period, character education defined by its conservative character and preservation of group norms, receded in the face of pluralism, iconoclasm , and "doing your own thing." Moral education, with all of its connotations of obligation, ebbed, to be replaced by values education. (According to those who espoused values clarification, values are not normative; they are matters of personal preference.) Values clarification, emphasizing the affective realm, replaced habituation and exhortation as methods of initiating the young into moral behavior. (Rather than answer the question, "Whose morals do we teach?" it was easier to advocate for none.)The goal of moral education shifted from transmitting norms and creating group affiliation to liberating the learner and teaching him or her to think about moral issues. Ethical questions rather than ethical actions dominated classroom discourse. Authenticity was eclipsed by relevance.

Moral education, as we have seen, includes the realms of thoughts, feelings, and action, or knowing the good, loving the good, and doing the good. The anti-transmission critics questioned the definitions of those terms (*what or whose thoughts, feelings, and actions?*), the source of the authority for the proper thoughts, feelings, and actions (*natural law, intuition, or God's revealed word?*), the valences assigned to each of the three categories (*which is most important?*), and the role of the teacher in moral education (*authority or facilitator?*). Traditional programs of moral education, whether based in schools or religious institutions, must be normative; their primary function is to transmit the vocabulary, literature, and values their societies identified as producing the good life. Traditional Jewish education consists of the choosing of moral virtues (Excellences) extracted from sacred texts and inculcating them through the interplay of Environment, Experiences, Expectations, and certain kinds of Exemplars (See Chapter 9 for a fuller treatment of this subject.) The system demands orthodoxy (right thinking or knowing the good) as well as orthopraxy (the right deeds or doing the good.)

Thoughtful "outside-in" Jewish educators have always hoped for the right feelings (loving the good), but surely do not begin their educational efforts in the affective realm, as do the transformative, "inside-out" pedagogues. The role of the "outside-in" teacher is to induct the learner into a culture based on canonically-sanctioned Excellences, not to help him discover himself. The belief that education, whether religious or secular, should appeal to the learner's reason, should be relevant, and should meet her needs, is one that emerged since the Enlightenment and flourished in the Vietnam era. Modernity, according to one of its chief analysts, is characterized by a world-view dominated by pluralism and secularism (Berger, 1990); transmission-type education does not thrive in a climate which denies that objective truth is independent of the knower. This modern sensibility reflected by the critics of traditional, transmission-centered education, posits that right thinking (accepting the creed and canons of the group) is less important than finding one's own way; that right behavior (behaving according to the norms of the group) is less important than behaving in ways which are consonant with one's personal philosophy, that the process of thinking about thorny moral issues takes precedence over its product—proper behavior. The role of the teacher, in their view, is to serve as a facilitator or coach, to "light lamps" rather than to "fill vessels."

The transmission backlash, the shift to the transformative, was felt in both Jewish and general educational circles. Jewish educators, along with their counterparts in American public schools, began to move away from their traditional role as agents of the community to a newer role as advocates for the individual. The "outside-in approach" was labeled as indoctrination—force-feeding ideas against the learner's will. Raths, Harmin, and Simon (1966), citing psychologists Peck and Havighurst, capture the zeitgeist which promoted values clarification instead of character education:

> *It is temptingly easy and insidiously gratifying to "mold" children, or to "whip them into line" by exercising one's superior status and authority as an adult. It is often personally inconvenient to allow children time to debate alternatives, and it may be personally frustrating if their choice contradicts one's own preferences. If there is any selfish, sensitive 'pride' at stake, it is very hard for most adults to refrain from controlling children in an autocratic manner. Then, too, like any dictatorship, it looks 'more efficient'—to the dictator, at least. However, the effect on character is to arrest the development of rational judgment and to create such resentments as prevent the growth of genuine altruistic impulses. For thousands of years, the long-term effects have been ignored and sacrificed to short-term adult advantages, most of the time. Probably it is no accident that there are relatively few people who are, or ever will become, psychologically and ethically mature."* (pp. 45-46)

Is the transmission approach de facto indoctrination? If indoctrination means transmitting the doctrines of a religious tradition, then is all religious education indoctrination? Rosenak (1983) poses that question and answers it. He acknowledges that both the method of religious education, the "outside-in" approach, makes it suspect, as does the content (revealed doctrines), and the intent (to shape the learner's thinking and behavior.) (pp. 119-121) But Rosenak points out that all of the charges leveled at religious education could be leveled at general education as well, even education in its most democratic, progressive forms. One look at Lawrence Cremin's (1977) definition of education proves Rosenak's point. Cremin, who wrote the definitive history of progressive education in America, defines all education as "the deliberate, systematic and sustained effort to transmit, evoke or acquire knowledge, attitudes, *values*,(italics mine) or sensibilities as well as the outcome of that effort." (p. 134) Therefore, education in any form is values education and thus could wrongly be construed as indoctrination.

In a more recent essay, Efron (1996) deals with the question "Is

Jewish education indoctrination?" She distinguishes between traditional moral education or character education which is indoctrination (transmission without inquiry) and Jewish education which is not. She concludes that since Judaism believes in free will, it cannot be indoctrination. "In traditional Jewish moral education emphasis is placed on the development of critical moral thinking skills that ensure a continuing creative and analytical interpretation of tradition." (pp. 11-12) (I find that the Efron tips the balance of the three critical dimensions of moral education, thought, feeling and action, far too much towards thought. We have seen that classical Jewish education, like any traditional system of moral education, is ultimately concerned with behavior. *Na'aseh* after all, does precede *nishma.*)

Israel Scheffler's (1995) clarification of the differences between religious education and indoctrination seem to be the most useful in providing educators with an early-warning alert, an anti-indoctrination alarm. He says that when teaching, even "outside-in teaching," i.e., classical Jewish education of the transmission variety, is accompanied by explanation, it cannot be called indoctrination. Explanation allows the teacher to present reasons for why Jews do what they do and believe what they believe. Explanation also gives the learner the context she needs to assimilate the norms and the habits of her community; those beliefs and rituals can be made meaningful through discussion. Explanation is not only the preserve of the teacher, but the property of the student as well. It allows the learner to explore what he or she believes and why. The Talmud is characterized by the verbal exchanges in which the rabbis explain their views; it was the exercise of explaining to the other which sharpened the study partner's wits. Responsa literature consists of questions and answers—explanations so that the questioner would understand the law. Explanation then is part and parcel of the most traditional forms of Jewish education.

Martin Buber discussed the role of Explanation within in a teacher's repertory of strategies. "For educating characters you do not need a moral genius, but you do need a man (sic) who is wholly alive and able to communicate himself directly to his fellow beings." When that connection is made, the student "accepts the educators as a person. He feels he may trust this man , that this man is... taking part in his life, accepting him before desiring to influence him. And so he learns to ask." Buber's attitude was that before there could be teaching, there had to be a relationship. When the teaching takes place, it is not about absolutes. "What the teacher should do is "to answer a concrete question, to answer what is right and wrong in a given situation." (Buber, 1965, pp. 105-107)

So how do we moderns balancing the twin goals of transmission and transformation deal with the ever-so-concrete, ever-so-troubling, question of *hiyuv* (obligation)? Buber's first answer would be to start with a loving relationship with our students, an I-Thou and not an I-It, relationship. Then we offer some Explanations for the *mitzvot*, make as rational a case as we can, and—then be prepared for some of our students to respond with questions of their own. They may offer their Explanations—for acceptance and rejection of the *mitzvot*. We as educators must be prepared to listen, to truly engage in dialogue, and also be prepared for our students to reject our Explanations—without rejecting our students.

Although Explanation might be more necessary in our skeptical era than in the past, it has always played an important role in Jewish teaching. Explanation is the force behind midrash; in fact, it fuels the engine of exegesis upon which rabbinic Judaism is based. A literature grew up around the reasons for observing the *mitzvot*, *ta'amei ha-mitzvot*. A leading scholar of Conservative Judaism, Elliot Dorff (1989), has written a wonderful book in this genre, Mitzvah Means Commandment. The section which follows is a summary of Dorff's review of the *ta'amei ha-mitzvot* literature.

Biblical reasons include reward and punishment, both Divine and human:

> *"If you follow My laws and faithfully observe My commandments, I will grant your rains in their season, so that the earth*

> *shall yield its produce and the trees of the field their fruit....And if, for all that, you do not obey Me, I will go on to discipline you sevenfold for your sins, and I will break your proud glory. I will make your skies like iron and your earth like copper....*" (Leviticus 26: 3-4, 18-19)

> *"When a man gives money or goods to another for safekeeping, and they are stolen from the man's house, if the thief is caught, he shall pay double."* (Exodus 22: 6-7)

Other Biblical explanations for the *mitzvot* include the fact that they have stood the test of time as an enduring source of wisdom. "Happy is the man who finds wisdom, the man who attains understanding. Her value in trade is better than silver, her yield, greater than gold." (Proverbs 3: 13-14) Yet another is that the *mitzvot* encapsulate the central principles of human morality: "The teaching of the Lord is perfect, renewing life; the decrees of the Lord are enduring, making the simple wise. The precepts of the Lord are just, rejoicing the heart; the instruction of the Lord is lucid, making the eyes light up." (Psalms 19: 8-9) Another Biblical explanation for the *mitzvot* is that we are part of that Covenant made at Sinai. Just as we imagine ourselves to be part of the throng which was redeemed from Egypt, we imagine ourselves to be at the base of the mountain, receiving God's revelation. We made a commitment at that time: God would protect us and give us the land of Israel if we would recognize God and keep God's *mitzvot.*

> *Yet, even then, when they are in the land of their enemies, I will not reject them (the people Israel) or spurn them so as to destroy them, annulling My covenant with them: for I the Lord am their God. I will remember in their favor the covenant with the ancients, whom I freed from the land of Egypt in the sight of the nations to be their God: I the Lord.* (Leviticus 26: 44-45)

Being a partner in a Covenant with God requires us to protect God's name by acting worthy of God's trust in us. The *mitzvot* help us to act in a moral fashion.

You shall faithfully observe my commandments: I am the Lord. You shall not profane My holy name, that I may be sanctified in the midst of the Israelite people—I the Lord who sanctify you, I who brought you out of the land of Egypt to be your God, I the Lord. (Leviticus 22: 31-33)

Differentiating us from the rest of the world, the Covenant is a path to holiness. Whereas the other nations are required to observe only the basic elements of morality (the Noahide laws), we are required to observe all of God's commandments. This responsibility helps us to become "a kingdom of priests and a holy nation." (Exodus 19: 6) Our relationship with God has also been described in terms of a special love, like that of man and wife. "And I will wed you forever: I will wed you with righteousness and justice, and with goodness and mercy. And I will wed you with faithfulness; Then you shall be devoted to the Lord." (Hosea 2: 21-22)

The rabbis added to the Biblical core of explanations for observing God's laws. Among them were the idea that the *mitzvot* make us more sensitive. "The commandments were given to refine God's human creation." (B'reishit Rabba 44: 1, as quoted by Heinemann, 1953, p. 25) Making a blessing before we eat transforms something mundane like eating into something holy. It teaches us not to take our abundant food for granted. *Kashrut* makes us aware of the sanctity of all life. The *mitzvot* also civilize the world. "God said, 'If you read the Law, you do a kindness, for you help to preserve My world, since if it were not for the Law, the world would again become 'without form and void...'" (Deut. Rabbah, Nitzavim 8:5) The *mitzvot* help make us a people apart by shaping our national character. *Kashrut* is the Jewish way of eating; the obligation to pray three times daily gives Jewish life its special rhythm, as do the advent of Shabbat and the holidays.

"Yet for all that, in spite of their sins, when they have been in the lands of their enemies, I have not rejected them utterly." (Leviticus 26:44) All the good gifts that were given them were taken from them. And if it had not been for the Book of the

Law which was lift to them, they would not have differed at all from the nations of the world. (Sifra 113a)

The rabbis proffer another explanation for the performance of *mitzvot*: the commandments add an esthetic dimension to our lives (*hiddur mitzvah.*) Surrounding ourselves with beautiful ritual objects like *tallitot*, *seder* plates, *hanukkiyot*, and *tzedakah* boxes elevates our spirits. As Dorff (1989) says, "The reason for these rules, of course, was to honor God and the occasion, but their effect (even if not their motive) was to make observance of these events enjoyable to all who participated." (p. 165) This is that affective realm we educators recognize as essential in creating a moral imagination—in nurturing students who "love the good."

Any discussion of God's rules is a perfect lead-in to discussing rules in other settings: why we do things this way in this classroom, in this school, and in this community. It gives the "*d'rash*" on the *p'shat* of school tradition. ("Why can't we eat in our classroom?" "Why do we have to invite everybody in the class to a birthday party?") The image of a loving God looking out for the well-being of God's people is an enormously powerful one. To use this language, so central to our thinking about rules and authority, recasts us educators in God's image. As parents and teachers, we explain that we do not allow children to play in the street; run with scissors in their hands; call others names, and so forth. We have rules. Why? Because we care about our children's well-being. We love them. This is the rationale for God's law, the explanation put forth in the evening liturgy:

With constancy You have loved Your people Israel, teaching us Torah and ***mitzvot****, statutes, and laws. Therefore, Lord our God, when we lie down to sleep and when we rise, we shall think of Your laws, and speak of them, rejoicing in your Torah and* ***mitzvot*** *always. For they are our life and the length of days; we will meditate on them day and night. Never take away Your love from us. Praised are You, Lord, who loves His people Israel. (Siddur Sim Shalom, 1985, p. 200)*

In reviewing the literature on parenting styles and moral education, Damon (1990) points out that children of authoritarian parents and children of laissez-faire parents often turn out to be quite similar; each group lacks moral grounding. The children of parents who set firm rules, who explain the reasons for the rules, and adhere to them consistently, tend to be more moral, i.e., more pro-social, more mindful of rules, and more skilled at moral reasoning. The parents of these children, whom Damon calls *authoritative* parents, have modeled basic elements of morality by linking rules and Explanation. Extending Damon's paradigm, God is therefore an *authoritative*, not an authoritarian, parent. The lesson we can draw from the *ahavat olam* prayer is that moral education is not indoctrination in laying out rules and insisting they be followed. It becomes indoctrination only when the rules are unaccompanied by Explanation, and when the learner is perceived as an object, an It. I first read Martin Buber's discovery of this truth when I was just beginning my career as a Jewish educator. Thirty years later, I am still profoundly moved by it.

> *When I was eleven years of age, spending the summer on my grandparents' estate, I used, as often as I could do it unobserved, to steal into the stable and gently stroke the neck of my darling, a broad dapple-gray horse. It was not a casual delight but a great, certainly friendly, but also deeply stirring happening. If I am to explain it now, beginning with the still very fresh memory of my hand, I must say that I experienced in touch with the animal was the Other, the immense otherness of the Other, which, however, did not remain strange like the otherness of the ox and the ram, but rather let me draw near and touch it. When I stroked the mighty mane, sometimes marvelously smooth-combed, at other times just as astonishingly wild, and felt the life beneath my hand, it was as though the element of vitality itself bordered on my skin, something that was not I, was certainly not akin to me, palpably the other, not just another, really the Other itself; and yet it let me approach, confided itself to me, placed itself elementally in the relation of Thou and Thou with me. The horse, even when*

I had not begun by pouring oats for him into the manger, very gently raised his massive head, ears flicking, then snorted quietly, as a conspirator gives a signal meant to be recognizable only by his fellow-conspirator; and I was approved.

But once—I do not know what came over the child, at any rate it was childlike enough—it struck me about the stroking, what fun it gave me, and suddenly I became conscious of my hand. The game went on as before, but something had changed, it was no longer the same thing. And the next day, after giving him a rich feed, when I stroked my friend's head he did not raise his head. A few years later, when I thought back to the incident, I no longer supposed that the animal had noticed my defection. But at the time I had considered myself judged. (Buber, 1965, pp. 22-23)

I return to Rosenak's wisdom—that religion and religious education must be authentic and relevant. In our efforts to make Jewish moral education authentic, I am concerned about those efforts which shortchange relevance, what rings true to a modern sensibility. The key to relevance is relationship, in E. M. Forster's felicitous rendering, "Only connect." That connection can be forged through Explanation.

HA-MA'ASEH

1. Explain classroom rules. Discuss your policies regarding the timeliness of assignments, absences, punctuality, the cleanliness of the room, and dress codes. Answering student questions does not erode your authority. If they feel a policy should be amended, invite them to make suggestions for change, and explain them in return. Create a process for student-involvement in rule-making.

2. Give students clear and sufficient feedback when evaluating their work. Demonstrate through your comments that you care about their progress and improvement. Remember: in Hebrew, the word for parents (*horim*) and teacher (*morah*) come from the same root. "He who teaches a child is as if he had created it." (Sanhedrin, 19b)

3. Talk to your students about why you teach. Share with them why

you think teaching is important for you as well as for the Jewish community. The professional and the personal are always intertwined. Explain your goals for moral education to parents as well as students. If you truly want them as partners in the enterprise of raising children who are good as well as smart, is to open a conversation with them. One way to do that is through explanation.

4. Don't fall back on "I'm the Mommy, that's why" reasoning. Offer explanations that appeal to your audience, without destroying the integrity of the tradition. The silencing pronouncement that "It's written in the Torah" has limited force with students and parents alienated from Jewish tradition. Franz Rosenzweig's thoughts on this subject ring as true today as they did seventy years ago:

> "A new learning is about to be born—rather, it has been born. It is a learning in reverse order. A learning that no longer starts from Torah and leads into life, but the other way round: from life, from a world that knows nothing of the Law, or pretends to know nothing, back to the Torah. That is the sign of the time." (Rosenzweig, 1955, p. 98)

5. A traditional insight into the I-Thou relationship which undergirds Buber's rationale for Explanation can be found in Pirke Avot. "Who is honored? One who honors everybody, as it is said, 'For those who honor Me I shall honor, and they who despise Me will be treated as of no account' [1 Sam. 2:30]" (Pirke Avot 4:1) Like Peters, who reflected on the paradoxical relationship of habit and reason, the framers of this *perek* understood that in the act of what appears to be giving up authority, the teacher actually gains it.

6. Be sure to teach the *Ahavah Rabbah* or *Ahavat Olam* to your classes, not only as part of the liturgy, but as a rationale for the observance of *mitzvot*. I saw one of my students teaching this material to children who were in the second through fourth grades. Even the youngest understood that their parents set rules for them because they loved them and could extend the metaphor to God and God's creation.

7. There are lovely pieces of literature which can be taught regarding the concept of *hiddur mitzvah*, e.g., Sholom Aleichem's story of the *etrog* which is accessible both in English and in Hebrew.

8. Samuel Dresner's little volume on *kashrut* is useful in providing a sampler of the *ta'amei ha-mitzvot* literature. The *Jewish Dietary Laws: Their Meaning for our Time* is available from the United Synagogue of Conservative Judaism's Department of Education.

CHAPTER 8

EXAMINATION

We have seen that moral education includes three dimensions: moral feelings, moral behavior, and moral reasoning. Traditional Jewish education, and general education, for that matter, emphasize the first two elements. Feelings, or a moral imagination, are stirred through stories or spectacle which made Excellences (virtues) come alive. Students are habituated into moral behavior through an Environment rich in moral Experiences; they learn by doing. Revelation produced Torah which consists of *mitzvot*: how the Israelites were to live their lives. There is an objective truth in God's law. Hertz (1956) offers his commentary on Genesis 2:17, God's injunction not to eat of the tree of good and evil:

> *Man's most sacred privilege is freedom of will, the ability to obey or to disobey his Maker. This sharp limitation of self-gratification, this 'dietary law,' was to test the use he would make of his freedom; and it thus begins the moral discipline of man. Unlike the beast, man has also a spiritual life, which demands the subordination of man's desires to the law of God. <u>The will of God revealed in His Law is the one eternal and unfailing guide as to what constitutes good and evil—and not man's instincts, or even his Reason, which in the hour of temptation often calls light darkness and darkness light</u>* (emphasis added.) *(p. 8)*

Compare Hertz's skepticism of reason as a moral guide (so jarring to liberal ears) with the power of reason as noted by some of the founders of the values clarification movement. Rejecting the "three misleading M's" of character education (moralizing, manipulating, and modeling), they conclude:

> *Values cannot be taught. But the process for arriving at them can be. We can teach our children to examine life rationally, to understand that they usually have a range of possible*

decisions, to consider the consequences of those decisions, and to make their choices based on their awareness of the options and the consequences. Then we can help them learn how to scrutinize their lives to see whether they really are living according to what they say they value. We can impress upon them the importance of arriving at their own personal values—not impulsively, thoughtlessly, or under the influence of others—but through deliberate consideration. (Simon & Olds, 1977, p. 23)

Although traditional Jewish education doubted whether values (sic) could be taught, it never dismissed the process of Examination either. We have noted that although "*na'aseh*" (the doing) is given priority over "*nishma*" (the discernment), understanding, not blind obedience, was the legacy of the revelation at Sinai. Thus a program of Jewish education which omits moral reasoning or discernment distorts our covenant with God. To discern requires Examination, our sixth E.

Both traditional Jewish education and traditional general education (Wynne's "Great Tradition" [1986]) fall short in the dimension of moral reasoning. Authority, as noted by Hertz, is far more important than autonomy. The emphasis is heavier on the doing than on the discerning. Of course *yeshivot* were designed to produce scholars in rabbinic literature who could master the intricacies of Talmudic reasoning, but their framework was decidedly legal, and not moral. (Schimmel, 1983) The ethical implications of their legal studies were left to the family and community, not to the school. (If the *yeshivot* had excelled in the ethical-moral domain, we never would have had a Musar movement.) Let us not romanticize the *yeshivot*; the rigors of halakhic reasoning were always reserved for the elite. Jewish education for the masses, like general education in American public schools, traditionally emphasized the bottom line: skills and practices. That bottom line often became a list of rules. The "*nishma*" component, the "why" came too rarely. Transmission was more important than transformation; behavior more important than understanding; heteronomy (obedience) more important than autonomy; product (results) more important than process; Experience more important than Examination, authenticity more important than relevance.

Both the values clarification movement and Kohlberg's cognitive-developmental model of moral education were attempts to stand traditional moral education on its head: to make Examination primary. If students could learn to grapple with ethical dilemmas, if their reasoning skills could be improved, they would then be able to transfer those skills to the world beyond the classroom and live ethical lives. Kohlberg was in complete agreement with the values clarification school in being suspicious of character education. All of them claimed that the "bag of virtues" (Kohlberg, 1975) approach did not produce autonomous thinkers. By emphasizing Examination, they believed that they could produce young people who would be good when their teachers weren't looking.

As we have seen, values clarification and Kohlberg had their Jewish equivalents. Values clarification was the bread and butter of Jewish youth movement programming. Students would be presented with a series of issues or self-definitions and then have to decide where they stood. The process included the following steps (Simon and Olds, 1977):

1. Choosing, which consisted of exploring options, counting consequences, and freely choosing (the teacher served as a facilitator and refrained from expressing her opinions);
2. Cherishing or Prizing, which included accentuating the positive (framing the choice in positive, not negative language). and "the rooftop shout," publicly declaring one's choice;
3. Acting, translating one's choice into action, and repeating that action until it became a pattern (Critics of values clarification argued that this last step, action, was given short shrift. As a classroom strategy, values clarification emphasized "knowing the good" and "loving the good," and very little "doing the good.") (See Sommers, 1984; Wynne, 1986)

I recall vividly the identity exercise that seemed to pervade Jewish teen programming in the seventies. Participants had to decide which label best suited them: an American, a human being, a woman or man, or a Jew. They would go to an area in the room designated for each category, confer with others who chose as they did in order to create the most compelling defense of their position, and then debate their stands with the rest of the group. There are echoes of values clarification in Grishaver and Huppin's (1983) *Tzedakah, Gemilut Chasadim, and Ahavah: A Manual for World Repair*. In asking students to think through the relationship between *tzedakah* and *gemilut hasadim*, the authors ask their readers with whom do they identify: Marc Millionaire, Buddy Blindsight, Goody Kaufman, Tammy Telephone, Nasty Norman, Sammy Supermarket, Sylvia Scholarship, and Abe and Ruth Chevrah.

Although Kohlberg (1975) agreed with the values clarification school in its critique of traditional moral education, he found values education vapid and ineffective. Not all values were created equal. Clarifying one's values did not necessarily lead to moral growth. Building on the work of Dewey and Piaget, Kohlberg (1969) postulated three moral stages, divided into six levels

1. The pre-moral or pre-conventional stage in which there was no sense of being morally obligated to rules (children obeyed to receive rewards or avoid punishment or to gain something in return; "you scratch my back and I'll scratch yours;")
2. The conventional or heteronomous stage in which "right" meant obeying the rules set by the social order, whether to be a "good boy or good girl" or to maintain group norms: "what if everybody did what he or she wanted to do?"
3. The post-conventional or autonomous stage when the rules are understood as abstract principles of justice, either as part of a social contract, to promote a healthy civil order, or as a categorical imperative, a universal moral obligation.

In Kohlberg's approach, the role of the teacher was not an impartial facilitator as in values clarification exercises, but a discussion leader committed to actively encouraging higher stage reasoning. Studies by Moshe Blatt in religious school classrooms led Kohlberg (1975) to believe that exposure to higher stages of moral reasoning through the analysis of moral dilemmas could move children up a stage on his developmental ladder.

Kohlberg's work was adapted by Earl Schwartz (1983) for Jewish schools. Schwartz explains to his teacher-readers that Kohlberg's priorities are perfectly consistent with those of classical Jewish thinkers. In order to make his case, Schwartz relies on Maimonides, the most rational of Jewish thinkers, as his "rebbe." In comparing Kohlberg to Maimonides, Schwartz finds the following areas of agreement:

1. Reasoning is an essential part of moral behavior;
2. Human beings pass through stages of moral development;
3. There is a correspondence between a child's age and his or her stage of moral development;
4. There is a trajectory for moral development from extrinsic to intrinsic rewards. (p. 15)

Some of the moral issues Schwartz includes in his book are reward and punishment, intentions, a good name, gossip or slander, deception, revenge, and justice and mercy. His technique is to develop moral judgment in students through the presentation of a dilemma and through guided exploration. This is the sixth E, Examination. The process culminates with the study of what traditional Jewish sources have to say on the issue.

Kohlberg, like Raths and Simon, the fathers of values clarification, are names rarely heard today in moral education circles. It is sad, but no surprise, that Schwartz's important book is no longer in print. Values clarification and the cognitive-developmental approach to moral development were social constructions, products of an era colored by rebellion against authority and convention. Their adherents inherited the inevitable backlash to the sea-change in values produced by the Vietnam War and its aftermath. Their hope was to de-emphasize product in favor of process, to substitute reason for rules, and thereby transform students into post-conventional, autonomous thinkers. Two decades later, the binary pull of American social history unleashed a backlash. Social and educational critics of the eighties and nineties blamed America's societal ills on the process-based, moral reasoning strategies of a decade or two before. Pedagogic materials that relied on Kohlberg or values clarification were pushed to the back of the shelves. Examination acquired a bad reputation, a straw man created by conservative critics, blamed for engendering the selfishness, violence, and decay imprinted on the moral fabric of American society.

Edwin Delattre, William Bennett's former classmate, denounced values clarification as follows: "Some programs, such as 'values clarification,' are based on a mindless reduction of morality to a matter of personal and arbitrary taste. Students are taught that whether you like genocide or bigotry is roughly the same as whether you like broccoli." (1992, p. 3) Others, lumping Kohlberg's work with values clarification, dismissed his approach as well; it became tarred by the same neo-conservative brush. One critic announced that he didn't care if his mugger did score a level five on Kohlberg's scale; he was still mugged. Reason was in retreat.

Kirschenbaum (See Simon, Howe, & Kirschenbaum, 1972), one of the most prolific authors of handbooks on values clarification in the seventies, became a proponent of character education in the nineties. (Kirschenbaum, 1995) Character education programs sprouted like mushrooms after the rain. Jewish education, taking its lead from general education, adopted *mitzvah* trees and lauded Jewish equivalents of Random Acts of Kindness. Before I am misunderstood, let me state unequivocally: I am most definitely in favor of good behavior—in myself, my children, my neighbor's children, my students, my politicians... (Do I need to go on?) Having made that confession, let me quickly add that programs based on "doing the good" alone will backfire. I worry, that in our current rush to repair behavior, we circumvent the issue of autonomy in favor of short term compliance. Alfie Kohn (1997) sums up the objections of the "inside-outside," transformative educators:

> *Let me get straight to the point. What goes by the name of character education nowadays is, for the most part, a collection of exhortations and extrinsic inducements designed to make children work harder and do what they're told. Even when other values are also promoted—caring or fairness, say—the preferred method of instruction is tantamount to indoctrination. The point is to drill students in specific behaviors rather than to engage them in deep, critical reflection about certain ways of being. (p. 429)*

The old bugaboo, indoctrination, resurfaces. As I have suggested in the previous chapter, one antidote to indoctrination is Explanation. A second is Examination. In our infatuation with binary models of thinking, we may have gone overboard in appealing to authority and banishing reason. The return of "The Great Tradition" has restored action and feeling to our classrooms, but often gives short shrift to Examination. I truly believe that for any approach to moral education to be effective, it must contain the three elements of action, feeling, and thought. In directing our appeal to heart and hand, we have often overlooked the head. To include all three elements, a teacher has to seek out opportunities to infuse the curriculum with occasions for moral deliberation about the Excellences which frame the life of the school community. Four such opportunities, created by my former students and geared for learners of different ages, appear below. What makes them so rich is that they capture true moral dilemmas, instances in which principles, or excellences clash. (A dilemma between good and not-good is no moral dilemma at all.)

Rabbi Sharon Cohen suggests a lesson for intermediate grades based on the Noah narrative. Having taught the *p'shat*, the story line, she suggests role playing Noah and his neighbors. The students can improvise conversations or inquiries, such as, "Noah! What in heaven's name are you doing?" or the teacher can freeze the action and ask the characters to elaborate on what the spare text conveys. For example, the teacher turns to the child who plays Noah and asks: "Noah, what did you think after you heard God's message to you?" Another teacher query may be directed to a neighbor. "Fred, as Noah's neighbor, you are thoroughly confused by what is going on. What might you say to Susan, your buddy next door?" If the students overlook some of the moral elements in the story, it is up to the teacher to highlight them, in Kohlberg fashion, by asking Noah why he didn't argue with God on his neighbors' behalf, as did Abraham, or why he didn't warn his neighbors. The Noah narrative spotlights the "lonely man of faith," the person who does God's bidding but alienates himself from her community or social group. Rabbi Cohen suggests that a follow-up discussion be held in which students discuss the times in their lives in which they were faced with similar ethical dilemmas, like having to choose between upholding a rule and going along with a friend. (Depending on the group, this reflective element might be done through journals in order to protect privacy and promote more soul-searching.)

Rabbi Lewis Warshauer creates a Bible unit of three to five lessons for pre-Bar and Bat Mitzvah students utilizing a video clip from the movie High Noon. In it, the sheriff argues that he should stay in town to deal with the villains who are terrorizing the inhabitants, while the sheriff's wife insists that he should leave for her sake. Dividing the class into *hevrutot*, Rabbi Warshauer suggests that the groups discuss the following questions:

1. What are the sheriff's arguments? What are the wife's arguments?
2. What represents the good for the sheriff? For his wife?
3. Do they see each other's point of view? Why or why not?
4. What do you think is best for the sheriff? for the sheriff's wife? for the town? If you were the sheriff, what would you do? Why?

After the small group discussions, the teacher should reconvene the class and ask for group reports. She should pose the following questions:

1. Who is being just and how?
2. Who is being brave and how?
3. Are there times when family is more important than community? Community more important than family? When?

The deliberation based on High Noon forms the backdrop for discussion of the Abram-Sarai-Hagar story in Genesis 16:1-6. After a close reading of the text, Rabbi Warshauer suggests that the teacher ask the following questions to *hevrutot*:

1. What arguments can you make in favor of Sarai's actions? Abram's? Hagar's?
2. What characters try to understand and act on someone else's point of view? Who?
3. Sarai says, "The Lord decide between you and me." What do you think God wanted? Why do you think so?

Once again the teacher reassembles the class, asks for reports of the discussions, and highlights the moral issues in the narrative:

1. Who is being just and how?
2. Is anyone being merciful?
3. Are there times when a peaceful home is more important than every family member being treated fairly, or the reverse?

Rabbi Warshauer suggests that the unit close with a personal analysis, asking the students to think about their thinking, how they used moral deliberation in each narrative. He recommends that the students reflect on how these two stories might be similar to issues that they face in their own lives. Finally, he asks students what they learned about making judgments that they did not know before the unit.

Rabbi Carrie Carter has designed a lesson that might be a part of a Jewish history course or a course on the Holocaust taught in a camp setting. She begins by telling students about an actual event which took place in Auschwitz.

Rabbi Zvi Hirsch Meisels described a "selection" conducted by the Nazis at Auschwitz in which some 1400 boys of less than an arbitrary height were singled out for death. (Kirschner, 1985) Some camp inmates sought to ransom certain boys by bribing the guards. However, the guards would not release any boy without capturing another to take his place. This trading in lives went on throughout the day.

The father of one of these condemned boys, aware that his son could be ransomed only at the expense of another life, asked R. Meisels whether under the circumstances the Torah permitted a father to save his son's life. R. Meisels did not wish to render an explicit decision in a capital case, especially without access to books of law, the counsel of other rabbis, or the calm objectivity necessary to make such a ruling.

Still, R. Meisels wondered whether or not there might be some rationale for permitting ransom. The isolated block in which the boys were confined was guarded by Jewish inmates who presumably might refrain from the grave sin of condemning another boy in the place of a ransomed one. As long as the exchange had not occurred, it might be permissible for the father to ransom his son on the assumption that another boy might never be captured. However, it was the guards' procedure to capture a replacement before releasing a ransomed captive, nullifying this line of argument.

Reluctant to render a defective halakhic ruling (*pesak din*), especially in such a calamitous circumstance, R. Meisels refused to answer the father's question. From the rabbi's refusal, the father concluded that the ransom of his son was halakhically forbidden.

On the same day, R. Meisels was approached by a boy seeking to ransom a young man who was a superior student of Torah. R. Meisels replied that the ransom was forbidden since it would merely condemn someone else. The boy responded that he wished to offer himself as a substitute. R. Meisels prohibited this also, since in the case of mutual extremity the preservation of one's own life takes precedence. (Kirschner, 1985, pp. 112-113)

Rabbi Carter recommends that the teacher highlight the moral dilemma of personal vs. communal responsibility, asking the students to give their rulings and responses to the decision rendered by R. Meisels. She would compare his ruling to the discussion in Mishnah Gittin 4: 6 on ransoming captives. Moving from the Jewish sources to the students' experience, Rabbi Carter suggests that the students write down an instance in which they had to choose between responsibility to a person and responsibility to the group. She adds that students might include their reflection in a journal; after the group discussion they might rethink their dilemma: Would they respond differently in light of the class discussion? Converting moral thinking to moral action, Rabbi Carter concludes by asking the group to come up with a list of activities they might take to ensure that their behavior at camp matched the values and ideals demonstrated in the text. She recommends posting the list for the duration of the summer, revisiting it as teachable moments occurred.

Drew Alexander designs a lesson based on role-plays for a high school in which the concept of *l'shon ha-ra* (harmful speech) has been part of a spiraling curriculum on the ethical *mitzvot*. In kindergarten it was introduced as a practical precept concerning student behavior, and the term was used in the context of disciplinary incidents as they arose. He draws on material in Tractates Yoma (9b) and Arakhin (15a -16b). In Drew's ideal school, students in the third grade study *l'shon ha-ra* in the context of the biblical stories of Miriam and Aaron's slander of Moses, the Ten Spies, and the Rashi on Exodus 2:14 (Moses' killing of the taskmaster.) In fifth grade they encounter *l'shon ha-ra* in the context of the liturgy of Yom Kippur. They subsequently study it in various rabbinic and medieval contexts. The purpose of this lesson is to reinforce in action concepts that students were already familiar with and to test their ability to apply what they had learned. They are engaged in truly examining what *l'shon ha-ra* is and what are its implications for modern teenagers.

The information in this role-play is progressively revealed in three steps. A core group of four or five students receives the information entitled, "Step One." One student is added in each subsequent step. Only these students see "Step Two" and "Step Three," respectively. After each step, the core group reacts for a few moments as actors in the drama engendered by the information they have received. The teacher stops the action by calling out "FREEZE!" and leads the entire class, including those who were not participants in the role-play, in discussion. After a ten minutes, the teacher can proceed to the next step. The role play begins with a narrator, chosen for his or her ability to read loudly and dramatically. The narrator serves as the voice of traditional Jewish texts. There is a concluding story which can be read, time permitting.

Narrator: Hear ye, hear ye!! *L'shon ha-ra* is a *"lo ta'aseh"* a "thou shalt not," or negative commandment!! It prohibits hurting another through words, spoken or written. It is based on the biblical verse "You shall not go about as a talebearer among your people." [Lev. 19:16] It says in the Talmud [Yoma 9b]: "Rabbi Elazar said: This [*l'shon ha-ra*] refers to people who eat and drink together and then thrust each other through with the dagger of their tongue!" *L'shon ha-ra*—evil speech—doesn't only refer to slander!! Let's see why!!

Step One

You all have a friend named Sally. You are standing around, just hanging out. One of you (decide among yourselves) starts the role-play by running in and announcing, "Oh my God!! I just heard that Sally was hugging and kissing this totally strange guy down at the train station!!" Now Sally has a boyfriend (Greg) that she has been going out with for a long time. He is also a friend of yours. Your job is to react to this news as you would in real life. How would you feel? What would you think and say about Sally? Her boyfriend? What would you want to do about it? Continue this discussion until you hear "FREEZE!!" Stay where you are at that point. Feel free to participate in the discussion. After the discussion the role-play will continue. Again, just react naturally to the new situation. Ask yourself the same questions—How would I feel, what would I think and say, what action would I want to take? You will hear "FREEZE!!" again and as before you should stay in place and participate in the discussion. There will be one more segment--a new character will come in--react as before. After the final "FREEZE!!" take a bow!! Thanks.

First Discussion

- What is the situation here? Did (student's name) do the right thing by spreading this information?
- How do feel about what you've learned?
- What did you decide to do as a result?
- Is this *l'shon ha-ra* that you've heard? Why or why not?

The teacher can turn to the narrator at any time during the discussion for the following pronouncement:

Narrator: The laws against *L'shon ha-ra* do not apply in cases where someone may be hurt as a result of their ignorance of the information or in cases where the information is public knowledge! But know this also—hearing *l'shon ha-ra* is no better than speaking it!!

The teacher can continue with additional questions:

- Is there a possible injury?
- Is this a case of public knowledge?
- How does this change things? Is this still *l'shon ha-ra*?

Second Step

You come running in with fresh news. You shout, "Hey, you guys!! That cute guy Sally was hugging was her cousin, and she only kissed him on the cheek!! BUT, Greg already broke up with her because he had heard she was kissing a strange guy!!" They will react to this information. Feel free to react to what they are saying but don't add to the information you've already given. If they press you for more details just say that's all you know. Thanks!

Second Discussion

• So much for the possible injury to the boyfriend. Where did the injury really come from? (not from NOT knowing something true that was potentially harmful, but by being harmed by something that was false)
• What does this news have to teach us about the nature of "public information"? (It could be public and still be wrong) How much can we rely on it?
• What course of action will you take now?

Again, the teacher should turn to the Narrator for the following information:

Narrator: The laws of *l'shon ha-ra* apply regardless of the truth of the information given. Even positive statements about a person can cause problems and fit into the category of *l'shon ha-ra*!

• Does that make you feel better or worse? (Better because the new information [that made you feel so bad] didn't make things worse with respect to *l'shon ha-ra* or worse because you've been guilty of *l'shon ha-ra* the whole time?)
• What will you do now? Do you owe Sally an apology? Can you fix this?

Third Step

You are Sally. You come upon this group of your friends and say, "Hi!" Wait for them to respond. After they answer, say "Look, I know you guys have been talking about me, but I don't care because I planned the whole thing. You know I've been going out with Greg like FOREVER, and I wanted to dump him, but I just didn't want to deal with it, you know? So I picked this cousin up at the train, and I don't really like him, I mean I barely even KNOW him, but I saw some girls from the field hockey team watching me, and I got like this great idea. So I hugged him and kissed him on the cheek so they would THINK I was going behind Greg's back. Now I hear he's broken up with me, so I guess it worked. Thanks!!" Now you walk away. Good job!

Third Discussion

• This turned out to be a real mess, didn't it? How do we feel about Sally?
• How did this *l'shon ha-ra* affect her?
• What about Greg? What was the effect on him? Is he better off in the long run?
• If so, does that make the *l'shon ha-ra* okay? Why or why not?
• What about us? How do we feel?
• You may have noticed that one effect of *l'shon ha-ra* is to make things happen that wouldn't otherwise have happened. For example, Greg wouldn't have broken up with Sally without the help of the field hockey team. What states of mind are likely to be prone to *l'shon ha-ra*? (boredom or needing to feel powerful)
• What are some ways to cut down on *l'shon ha-ra*? (Avoid using names as much as possible, or disguising situations by changing details.) Be aware of what you know, don't know, and the source of your information. Consider that there are consequences that you might not be able to predict and that things aren't always what they seem .

A Story

(If there is time)

One day a man approached the Chofetz Chaim, a great rabbi who wrote a very important book devoted to *l'shon ha-ra*, and told him something very negative that he had heard about a person. The Chofetz Chaim said, "Once a man told me that he saw a man dancing with a female who was not his wife on Tisha b'Av, a fast day, a day of mourning and great sadness. Upon investigation, it turned out that the female was his infant daughter and because Tisha b'Av fell that year on Shabbes, the fasting and mourning was postponed until the next day. The man was filled with the joy of Shabbes and the miraculous life of his beloved child." The man face grew very red and he turned and walked away without saying a word.

For Deeper Study

(If there is time)

The following could be presented as a handout for homework or done collectively using the blackboard, in a subsequent class, depending on the class response to the role-play.

> *L'shon ha-ra* is actually a generic term which can be broken down into three groups. There is *rekhilut*, which is more like gossip, speech, or even gestures which, whether true or not, negative or not, causes hatred. For example: Person A says something to person B which causes them to hate person C. If it is also disparaging (negative) then it becomes also *l'shon ha-ra*. But *l'shon ha-ra* in the strict use of the term only applies if the statement is true. For example: Person A says, "Person B stole-(at this point, if true, it is *l'shon ha-ra*)-your pen."Now it is *rekhilut* because you now hate Person B. *Motzi shem ra* is the third term. This is pure slander, a disparaging statement one makes about someone knowing it to be false. (See Marchant, 1998)

Try to sort out the different occurrences of *l'shon ha-ra* in the role-play, determining which is r*ekhilut*, which is *l'shon ha-ra*, and which is *motzi shem ra* in the following examples:

- The girls' field hockey team spreads the story.
- Greg breaks up with Sally and tells his friends about it.
- "I just heard that Sally was hugging and kissing this totally strange guy..."
- "That guy Sally was with was her cousin, and she only kissed him on the cheek!"
- "I hugged and kissed him on the cheek so they would think..."

All four lessons try to create opportunities for critical thinking about dilemmas. However, unlike values clarification, in each case the lessons are tied to tradition, a tradition that privileges the authority of the past, by being anchored in Jewish Excellences, while still respecting the students of the present who cannot leave their questions behind when they enter the doors of their Jewish schools. As Burton Cohen (1984) noted, Jewish education does its students a disservice when it fails to teach what Aristotle called the "practical" disciplines. The practical disciplines require teaching the skills necessary to lead one's life according to informed choices. Building opportunities for examination into the curriculum attends to the "practical" discipline. As teachers, we always hope for that "transfer of training"—that the skills we teach will transfer from the classroom to the wider world.

A caveat: having prepared lessons, even skillfully designed and engagingly presented ones like those above, is not enough. Comedian Elaine May is reputed to have quipped, "I like a moral problem so much better than a real problem." Teachers should use real problems as well as hypothetical ones in order to refine their students' Examination skills: an outbreak of graffiti in the building, bullying on the playground, or students who act rudely in synagogue while attending the *b'nai mitzvah* ceremonies of their classmates. What happens outside the formal curriculum—those teachable moments, the unplanned, spontaneous events that grow organically out of school life—provide stunning opportunities for instruction and practice in "knowing the good."

HA-MA'ASEH

1. Bring the news into your classroom, highlighting the ethical decisions which must be made. Ask the students to look at dilemmas in the Jewish world, in the American community, and in their neighborhoods from multiple vantage points. Unfortunately, the news from Israel is full of opportunities for discussions based on the conflict between two "goods."

2. Kohlberg created "the just community" so students could practice the habits of deliberation. Have your students discuss and promulgate classroom rules and propose responses to theft, violence, and vandalism in the classroom and in the school.

3. Teach what Parker (1997) calls the deliberative arts in your classroom: listening as well as talking, taking turns, striving to

understand an other's point of view, criticizing the idea and not the person, admitting ignorance, asserting an unpopular view, and supporting a position with evidence. (p.20)

4. Reframe Bible courses so that the central theme is one of our forefathers and foremothers dealing with ethical dilemmas. Such a course might include the eating of the fruit of the Tree of Knowledge; Abraham & Sodom; Abraham, Sarah, and Avimelekh; the Akedah; Rebecca, Jacob, and the birthright; Judah and Tamar; Joseph and his brothers at the pit and in Egypt; Esther and Ahasuerus; etc.

5. Use ethical dilemmas as the narrative thread for a course in Jewish history. You might include the decision of Spanish Jews to become conversos, R. Meir Berlin's decision to close the *yeshivah* of Volozhin rather than allow it to be russified, the decision of the Irgun to blow up the King David Hotel, and whether Federations should direct funds to the affiliated or to marginal Jews.

6. Jewish responses to medical ethical dilemmas are very popular with teenagers and their parents. A Jewish family education course might include texts on birth control, abortion, euthanasia, and making medical decisions with limited resources.

7. Include a reflective component in *tikkun olam* experiences. In the Epstein School in Atlanta, students are asked to keep a diary in which they examine their feelings as they visit the elderly and celebrate holidays with them, create artwork for homeless shelters, work with special needs children, and distribute food in a food bank. Until students take the time to deliberate about what these experiences mean to them, they haven't dealt with the Examination dimension which is critical in any program of moral education. (Although the Epstein School asks that the journals be kept in English, an occasional entry might be made in Hebrew as well, affording yet another opportunity for moral education across the curriculum.) Their *Na'aseh v'Nishma* rabbinics curriculum is a jewel.

Chapter 9

Exemplars

The previous chapter dealt with the intellectual dimension of moral education. This chapter is about the affective dimension, the creation of a moral imagination. This is yet another aspect of *kavanah*, or motivation, what Aristotle called "loving the good." What causes one to want to do the good? Kohlberg and the values clarification school believed that it was knowing what was the ethically right thing to do. But many moral theorists, including our own Rabbi Israel Salanter, the father of the musar movement, doubted the power of reason. (Etkes, 1993) He was convinced that the cerebral realm, or knowledge of the good, had its limitations. One can discern what the moral course is and still not take it. We all know people, including ourselves, who know what the right thing is and still don't do it. What provides the inspiration for doing the right thing?

One way of fueling a moral imagination is through vivid examples of courage, integrity, and justice. Rules and reason do not galvanize like experience and example. Pascal's famous aphorism, "The heart has its reasons that reason doesn't know," rings true to us. We become moral individuals because of our grandparents, our teachers, and powerful models from literature and history.

> *We develop our moral sense because of how people have treated us, what we have experienced and the moral ideals and frames our culture supplies us. Our moral understanding is build up around the moral prototypes we have encountered and the meaning they have for us. We are inspired by the lives, either actual or fictional, of people who seem to us to be caring, sensitive, intelligent, courageous and wise. We get a sense of what we might become and how we might live by observing how they live and by trying to act as they would in a given situation.* (Johnson, 1993, p. 258)

What compels us about these figures is the story they live out in their lives. Yeats notes that we can't tell the dancer from the dance; we can't separate the Exemplar from his or her story. The power of the narrative in education and psychology is well known. (Bruner, 1986; Sarbin, 1986) You recall all the times you created mnemonics in order to memorize senseless lists. Stories help us learn. The role of narrative in moral education is just beginning to be understood. Researchers capture the recollections of individuals who listen for the stories of their moral authorities to help in their deliberations. These stories, not reason, are what inspire the desire to "do the good."

> ***Interviewer:*** *Is it fair to say then that the reasoning you've just described is what governed your action, your decision in this case?*
> ***Porter:*** *Actually no.*
> ***Interviewer:*** *No?*
> ***Porter:*** *No. What really clinched it was my grandfather.*
> ***Interviewer:*** *Your grandfather?*
> ***Porter:*** *Yes, he's deceased, but he was an extraordinarily important influence in my life, really the person to whom I looked for guidance. And you know, I realize that this could sound strange, you're a psychologist and so on, but, well, I have these conversations with him. That is, my grandfather is still there in the moral sense, as a presence to whom I turn and with whom I interact when I'm going through the kind of situation that I'm trying to describe to you.* (Day, 1991, p. 31)

What makes Porter do the right thing? He remembers his grandfather and the Excellences which his life embodied; Porter then "rehearses" (Porter's term) his decision with his grandfather as a critical audience. Would grandfather do it this way?

Although they didn't spell it out in the psychological language of our era, traditional "outside-in" educators have always depended upon literary and historical exemplars to symbolize the abstract virtues or Excellences which serve as group norms. The Greeks use stories of heroes to exemplify the virtues to which human beings were taught to aspire. Our stories embedded in Biblical and talmudic narrative do the same thing: What would *Avraham avinu* do? the great sages of the past? Transmission-type educators also acknowledge the importance of living Exemplars to provide the modeling necessary to help children or newcomers to acquire those norms. Society needs the influence of sterling individuals who mold by their everyday example: pious Jews whose lives are informed by *mitzvot*, Jews committed to social justice, and teachers whose ordinary demeanors are infused with moral significance. It is in the realm of the Exemplars that moral imaginations are crafted; it is in the realm of Exemplars that both transmission and transformation can take place.

Heroes: Classical, New, and Ordinary

Exemplars from oral or written tradition serve the didactic function of transmitting the moral values of the group. These classical heroes motivate through the power of narrative; whether they are real or fabricated does not matter. They are mythic, larger than life. Joan of Arc is the concretization of French nationalism; Paul Bunyan embodies the physical courage of the American frontiersman; Abraham, the much-vaunted *middah* of *hakhnassat orhim* (hospitality). Mere mention of their names conjures up all sorts of associations with a religious or national history and a vision of the future. These exemplars stir the moral imagination through the moral values they stand for: Abraham who would follow God anywhere, including heeding God's call to sacrifice his son; Paul Bunyan who felled the dense forests of the Midwest with his giant axe and his blue ox, Babe, a tribute to the perseverance and courage of 19th century settlers; Joan of Arc who would die at the stake for a vision of a France free of English invaders. The function of the classical exemplar, the Hero with a capital H, like that of the flag or national anthem, is to provide the social and emotional glue for a community.

The medieval French commentator Rashi explores the connection between the Hero and the community when he puzzles over Genesis 28:10: "And Jacob went out from Beersheba and went towards Haran." Why couldn't the text have been more concise—"And Jacob went towards Haran." Why the seemingly extraneous words "from Beersheba?" Rashi responds to his own question by noting: "It (Torah) intends to tell us that the departure of a righteous person from his city makes an impression. As long as a righteous man is in his city, he is its glory and splendor and beauty; when he leaves it, there departs also its glory, its splendor and its beauty." These Heroes are the ancestor portraits which we hang proudly above our metaphorical mantels. It is to them we point when we wish to train our young and bring newcomers into the fold. We remember and re-member—reconnect with our group's history and our group's destiny.

The Hero, the "outside-in" exemplar, must be distant and remote to do his or her work. In traditional Jewish circles, the hero, called a *godol* , is on a higher plane, or *madreigah*, than you or I. It does not matter that his feats are not "real;" they are no less "true." As Ahad Ha-Am (1912) muses regarding Moses,

> *...I do not grow enthusiastic when the dragnet of scholarship hauls up some new 'truth' about a great man of the past; when it is proved by the most convincing evidence that some national hero, who on in the hearts of his people, and influences their development, never existed, or was something absolutely unlike the popular picture of him. On such occasions I tell myself: all this is very fine and very good, and certainly this 'truth' will erase or alter a paragraph of a chapter in the book of archeology; but it will not make history erase the name of its hero, or change its attitude towards him, because real history has no concern with so-and-so who is dead, and who was never seen in that form by the nation at large, but only by antiquarians; its concern is only with the living hero, whose image is graven in the hearts of men, who has become a force in human life. (p. 307-308)*

The Hero's exploits represent the story of the people as they wish it to be told. It matters not to Ahad Ha'am that Moses may not have done what Torah purports him to do. Canon builds community. Another community-builder is history. The American common school relied on stories about the Founding Fathers; my Jewish education included a large component of modern Jewish history: stirring stories of those who built the state of Israel: Theodor Herzl, David Ben-Gurion, Golda Meir, Mickey Marcus, and Moshe Dayan.

The cultural revolutions of the 1960's and 1970's produced massive societal changes. The emergence of feminism and pluralism resulted in shifting definitions of moral exemplars. Both Jewish schools and American public schools tried to respond to the demand for a more diverse set of Heroes with a capital H. New heroes, including women and people of color, penetrated the phalanx of white, generally male, exemplars. Golda Meir and Hannah Senesch are well-known examples. Another is Gracia Nasi, a 16th century Sephardic woman who supported Jewish scholarship, organized the first boycott to rectify the injustices leveled at other Jews, and supported the rebuilding of the land of Israel, one of the New Heroes used by Jewish teachers to inspire the young to study, fight for social justice, and support the state of Israel.

Besides inheriting a legacy of pluralism and feminism, the post-Vietnam generation also acquired a spirit of iconoclasm. Patriotism became suspect, and with it, the classical Heroes of a simpler era. Presidents, statesmen, and military heroes were fair game for the revisionists. It is sad that today Jefferson is more likely to be remembered for his alleged affair with the slave Sally Hemmings than for his contributions to the founding of the United States; that Yonatan Netanyahu's heroism is now labeled a fabrication. Even though Heroes are human, and therefore innately flawed, the times demanded the unattainable, the oxymoron of a perfect Hero. Iconoclasm bred negativism: Better no hero than a flawed one, most Americans thought.

For others reeling from the social revolutions of the sixties, iconoclasm led to downsizing, the emergence of the hero with a small h, the "ordinary," or "local hero." (Yet another oxymoron.)

Instead of the extraordinary, timeless heroes of Carlyle and the Bible, the new moral exemplars became the good folk who struggled to make their communities better places by battling urban blight, racism, and ugliness. As a Jewish educator, I have noted a similar process; like the innards of our calculators and laptops, Jewish heroes have become miniaturized. To paraphrase the late Speaker of the House, Tip O'Neill, all heroes are now local. Mitzvah programs, inspired by Danny Siegel's work (1993), or Jewish adaptations of The Giraffe Program (1991) concentrate on "real life heroes—men, women and children worthy of admiration and emulation." (p. iii) Everyday saints, if you will. The real-life hero could be you or me if we were committed to the ideal of *tikkun olam*.

Role Models: Old and New

A fourth type of moral Exemplar is the role model. Although New Heroes and ordinary heroes are expressions of recently changed norms, the role model has always been used in traditional moral education. Holy men, *tzaddikim*, were meant to be observed by their followers. Even the smallest details, like how they tied their shoes, served to illuminate the path to an ethical and religious life for their disciples. In addition to the religious virtuosi, the transmission school has always depended upon parents and teachers to serve as role models: to teach the young what behaviors the community expects of its adult members. Our task as Jewish educators is complicated by the fact that many parents do not know what is expected of them. In addition, many teachers in Jewish schools, like Charles Barkley in the now-famous television commercial, do not want to be role models.

If that is the case, then some career counseling is in order. To paraphrase Purpel and Ryan (1976), "moral education comes with the territory." Durkheim theorized that teachers are secular priests, agents of the community which expects them to serve on its behalf. "Just as the priest is the interpreter of his god, the teacher is the interpreter of the great moral ideas of his time and of his country." (Durkheim, 1956) Everything a teacher does conveys moral messages; this is what one Talmudic sage meant when he said, hyperbolically to be sure, that a scholar who goes out in public with a grease spot on his clothes is worthy of death. (Shabbat 114a)

With the ascendance of the transformation school of moral education, the function of moral education changed. Its goal was no longer producing group cohesion, but promoting self-esteem. The teacher was no longer thought of as the preserver of the social order, but a facilitator or coach whose primary responsibility was to help students in self-actualization. (This psychologization of education helped produce the values clarification movement and Kohlberg's cognitive-developmental system.) To find oneself requires role models.

Like "ordinary hero," role model is not quite the right term. Role models in traditional moral education literally teach social roles: for example, how one behaves as a Jew or an American. Like the contemporary usage of hero, the term role model has become muddied. When feminists or people of color call for more role models, they are not looking for exemplars to teach what the social order demands from its members. They are looking for the reinforcement of a positive self-image. Role models are personal; heroes are public. Whereas classical heroes are transcendent, beyond time and space, role models, like ordinary heroes, are immanent. They can live next door. (For a fuller analysis of the definition and function of moral exemplars in moral education, see Maps, Metaphors, and Mirrors [Ingall, 1997].)

Heroes, Role Models, and Celebrities

Chronicler of religion Kenneth Woodward (1990) describes Catholic saints, like Heroes with a capital H, as simultaneously serving as both objects of veneration and emulation. His insight illuminates another legacy of the Vietnam era. In dethroning classical heroes, the revisionists were left with only celebrities to venerate and emulate. Lasch (1978) attributes the fascination of the American public with the famous to a cultural artifact of an age of narcissism which began in the fifties. (In the *yeshivah* world, the cachet of the celebrity is transferred to great teachers of Torah.

Youngsters treasure Rebbe cards, trading cards featuring Torah scholars and their "stats.") In fact, our society has been tantalized by celebrities long before Barnum brought Jenny Lind to America. Nearly fifty years ago, Havighurst and Taba (1949) investigated adolescents' ideal selves. They asked their respondents to complete the phrase, "The person I would like to be like..." Celebrities or glamorous individuals were people sixteen year-olds wanted to emulate, along with parents, relatives, composite or imaginary characters.

These studies were replicated by Wechter (1981) as part of his doctoral dissertation. When he asked young people about their ideal selves or in Freudian terms, their ego ideals, he discovered that teenagers' images of the ideal self or ego ideal fall into four categories:

1. Parents or parent surrogates: teachers, family friends, grandparents
2. Glamorous adults: movie stars, athletes, and heroes
3. Attractive and successful adults within the individual's range of observation
4. Composite or imaginary characters: abstractions of a number of people (p. 65)

Children younger than eight were more likely to choose parents or parent surrogates as ego ideals; eight-to sixteen-year olds were apt to choose glamorous or famous adults or attractive, visible adults in the community.

Wechter's research has been corroborated by research on British and Australian young people. Celebrities wield enormous influence. However, the nature of this influence is unclear. It surely affects matters of taste and fashion. Does it shape moral thinking and action as well?

My own research, albeit with a small sample (Ingall, 1997), leads me to believe that middle school youngsters seem to compartmentalize the influence of celebrities. (I have not investigated who younger children and older teens look to as heroes and role models.) While young teens may admire glamorous celebrities and powerful athletes as arbiters of style, they still look to parents and significant adults, including teachers, as role models and moral Exemplars. Having said this, I cannot absolve the media from their responsibility in creating a moral desert regarding heroes and role models. If the media, particularly television, can sell advertising on the basis of television's power to influence consumption, then they cannot deny television's power of moral persuasion. The media cannot have it both ways: their influence must extend to matters of morality as well as the wallet.

What Jewish Schools Can Do

We cannot create total institutions (Goffman, 1961) which shut out anti-social influences by erecting impermeable boundaries. In the liberal Jewish community, our boundaries are all too porous. But rather than ignoring the music, movies, and television programs our students see and hear, we can discuss them in our classes, offering Jewish alternatives to Hollywood's values. (Price, 1995) We can examine the moral issues which are at their core, using Socratic dialogue, offering examples in how we live our lives, and through the redemptive voice of moral literature. Many schools have involved their families in banning television for a week and offering them alternatives like reading aloud, playing family games, and simply talking with one another.

I have mentioned it elsewhere, but it bears repeating: teachers must become more reflective about their responsibilities as moral exemplars. If our students notice when we've cut our hair or changed our glasses, why shouldn't they notice if we treat one of them rudely or behave in a petty fashion? Our responsibilities as moral educators mean negotiating that authenticity-relevance axis: preserving and transmitting our cultural heritage through classical heroes as well as providing images of positive Jewish role models (including ourselves.)

Eschewing *gedolim* in favor of "miniaturized heroes" comes

with a price. (I don't feel quite as strongly about this as Oscar Wilde. He is supposed to have mused that in the past we used to canonize our heroes. Today, we vulgarize them. Cheap editions of great books are wonderful, but cheap editions of great men are detestable.) In our attempts to make our moral exemplars accessible, to emphasize role models and ordinary heroes to the detriment of classical or new heroes, we neglect the building of a deep moral imagination. The epic has its place in nourishing awareness of one's moral growth by the standards of virtue it sets. Not only do we deprive our students of our people's "master stories" (Fowler, 1981), but we lose an opportunity to sensitize our students to what linguists like Whorf and Vygotsky call "thinking-dispositional behavior." (Tishman & Perkins, p. 372) The word precedes the thought: one can imagine the transcendence of the *godol* because there is a language for it. Students who are taught about heroes can imagine heroic behavior.

The stories of role models or ordinary heroes tend to be universal stories; they are not particularly Jewish stories. Good people can be found in every community, religious, and ethnic group. *Gemilut hesed* programs in our religious schools look remarkably similar to those in secular schools. As Fishman (1996) notes, contemporary, liberal American Jews tend to blur distinctions between Jewish and American values. The Jewish values currently prized by our schools, and exemplified by role models and ordinary heroes, like pulling one's self up by the bootstraps, feeding the hungry, and tending the earth, (all wonderful stories!) are those that fit neatly with American culture. But the Jewish master story is not the same as the American story. Bible and Jewish history offer stories of heroes and create connections to peoplehood, a peoplehood which makes us different, a holy nation and a kingdom of priests. In relying on the *mitzvah* hero, or the role model, we inadvertently replace Jewish particularism with universalism and impoverish our students by denying them access to the world of metaphor and symbol.

I suspect that the tide is turning, that Heroes with a Capital H may be returning. I have only anecdotal evidence; librarian friends tell me that biographies, once languishing on the shelves are now circulating; that new Jewish history books are being published; that holding a magnifying glass up to heroes to find their flaws is proving tiresome, that Bible study is returning to school curricula. I hope so. In the words of that great social commentator Will Rogers, "We can't all be heroes because someone has to sit on the curb and clap as they go by."

I suggest that Jewish moral education considers an approach that relies on both types of Exemplars, the Hero and the role model, a synthesis of the transcendent and the immanent. I offer the *Adon Olam* prayer as a paradigm. It portrays a multi-dimensional God, the distant Creator of the cosmos who is also a nearby, personal protector. By utilizing the entire spectrum of moral Exemplars, by restoring the balance between the transcendent and immanent, by fusing transmission- and transformation-based pedagogies, we not only help our students to individuate, but to identify as Jews as well.

HA-MA'ASEH

1. Recognize the fact that you as an educator are a role model, a moral Exemplar. You are always on view. Pick up paper in the halls; erase the blackboard for the teacher whose class follows yours. Rearrange the room before you leave. Don't badmouth colleagues or administrators. Treat students as you would wish to be treated. Smile! ("Greet everybody cheerfully"—B'rakhot 17a) You want to balance self-awareness with spontaneity: You can't be so hyper-aware of your moral responsibilities that you have lost the freedom to be yourself.
2. Highlight "ordinary heroes" in the news. Differentiate them from the heroes of Jewish history and of Jewish texts. If your language regarding moral Exemplars is precise, the chances are that your students' language will be precise also. If you clarify your students' language, you have a headstart on clarifying their thinking.
3. Read to your younger students about moral Exemplars: fables, biographies of great men and women, poems, and stories. For older children, choose literature that stands on its own as great literature, not didactic material that shrieks its moral message. Choose

examples that deal with moral complexity and ambiguity.

4. What does Pirke Avot 4: 1 mean by "Who is strong? (heroic) One who overcomes his desire, as it is said, 'He who is slow to anger is better than the mighty, and he who rules his spirit than he who takes a city.'" (Prov. 16:32) Why would such an interpretation be useful for a people in Diaspora? How have Jewish heroes changed over time?

5. Invite moral Exemplars to your class. Have them tell their stories in their own words. Meeting a local hero can be enormously inspiring. (Aaron Feuerstein, the man who kept his promise to his factory workers to rebuild after a crippling fire and who paid their salaries and benefits while he did so, made the round of Boston religious school commencements. The students were enchanted. Obviously you need to be selective. Choose someone who communicates well.)

6. Create a Jewish heroes Hall of Fame in your classroom or school. Have students define what a Jewish hero is and how their hero exemplifies those agreed-upon criteria. Let them install an exhibit in the classroom or school that explains their choices to others. Invite other classes, parents, and grandparents to visit your class's museum. Include an interactive log so visitors can nominate their choices for inclusion and why.

7. Offer a course for parents and teenagers on Jewish heroes. Have each family unit share their heroes, current and past, and research a hero both generations agree is a Jewish hero. Each family is required to teach a class to the others based on their hero.

8. Work with your faculty and board on the establishment of an annual television-free zone and how to fill the vacuum with activities which promote moral literacy. You may want to pair up with other schools in the community on this project and thus increase your influence.

CHAPTER 10

EMPATHY

Just as Exemplars play a substantive role in both "outside-in" and "inside-out" education, Empathy does as well. Just as Exemplars are key to the building of a moral imagination, so is Empathy. Mark Johnson describes empathy as "the ability to *imagine* ourselves in different situations and conditions at past and future times." (He emphasizes *ourselves*; I emphasize *imagine*. [1993, p. 199.]) Empathy is a fuzzy word; for some it is feeling what the other feels (Hoffman, 1976); for others it is intuiting the other's experience or state of mind. (Kagan, 1984) Regardless of the definition, the word Empathy evokes associations of perspective-taking, of caring for the other.

One of the reasons that Rabbi Israel Salanter was so successful in attracting disciples to his Musar movement was because of his extraordinary capacity for Empathy. His biographer (Etkes, 1993) relates two incidents which illuminate this quality:

> *When Rabbi Israel was asked (regarding the second day of* ***Rosh Hashanah*** *which happened to fall on a Friday, leaving little time for Shabbat preparation) which* ***piyyutim*** *they might skip, he answered: 'One may omit all of the* ***piyyutim****, even* ***U-netaneh tokef*** *(the dramatic highpoint of the service that describes the fear and trembling felt in anticipation of Divine Judgment), but for Heaven's sake, do not skip the* ***piyyutim*** *in* ***Mussaf*** *between* ***Malkhuyot, Zikhronot****, and* ***Shofarot****, so that the cantor can rest for a few moments. (p. 165)*

Etkes also shares with his readers the reminiscences of Rabbi Israel's son regarding his father. Salanter once attended a wedding which ended quite late. Recognizing the lateness of the hour, he decided to sleep over at the wedding hall rather than risking disturbing his neighbors by knocking on the door of his house. (p. 165)

Salanter's Empathy has been immortalized in David Frishman's story "Three Who Ate." The tale is set during a cholera epidemic raging through a Jewish community. The hero of the story, modeled after Rabbi Israel, was so concerned about the well-being of his congregants that he insisted, to their shock, that the *Yom Kippur* fast be suspended. To convince them to do so, he and his two *gabbayim* ate first. (The same moral feeling pervades the popular short story of Y. L. Peretz, "If Not Higher," in which the beloved rabbi of Nemerov disguises himself as a crude woodsman in order to provide fuel for an ailing old woman. The story is reminiscent of one told about Rabbi Israel Salanter who nearly missed the *Kol Nidre* prayers because he was tending to a crying child unheard by her exhausted older sister who was sleeping. [Goldberg, 1972])

It is Empathy which builds a bridge between God and God's people; by loving each other we imitate God. (One is reminded of the Hasidic question, "How does one learn to love God?" and the answer, "By practicing on His creatures.") We treat one another not merely as members of like-thinking, like-living people, but as members of one family, a family which needs the love of its members. Twentieth century Jewish theologians like Abraham Joshua Heschel (1956) and David Wolpe (1990) have explored the classical Jewish notion that even God has needs: God needs human beings, and God suffers. Just as God displays pathos to God's creatures, God's creatures must return the kindness by displaying Empathy to their fellow creatures.

Empathy also looms large in the literature of the psychology-inspired theorists who feel that the goal of moral education is not the preservation of the group, but individual transformation. For feminist critiques of Kohlberg responsibility to and for others is the goal of moral education. Caring, as it is usually called, has become a corrective to the justice-centered approach to moral education suggested by the cognitive-developmental school. In her famous critique, Gilligan (1982) points out that Kohlberg's male sample skewed his findings. For the neo-Kantian Kohlberg (1969), the highest level of morality is the autonomous individual who could stand apart from the group and do the just thing, no matter what the personal and social cost. Responses to Kohlberg's instruments based on obligations to others were deemed "conventional" responses, lower on his scale than the "post-conventional" ones. Gilligan contends that the women interviewed by Kohlberg and his associates were not normatively deficient because they did not value rights as did men. She claims that there are two voices of moral concern: one of justice and one of care. She wonders whether the highly contextual ("Well, in this set of circumstances...") responses given by women (and a smattering of men) which emphasized responsibilities to others are any less moral than the principled responses ("This is the right thing to do no matter what...") offered by predominantly male respondents. In Gilligan's view, connectedness to others is as much a moral desideratum as adherence to an abstract principle.

Gilligan's work has been challenged and criticized by many for both her research methodology, her conclusions, and their implications. Walker (1984) demonstrates that women are not outscored by men on Kohlberg's scale; as they move up the social and economic ladder, they respond like their male counterparts. Faludi (1991) claims that Gilligan has inadvertently created an anti-feminist backlash by evoking echoes of biological determinism. Despite this criticism, Gilligan's views have made caring a staple of moral education across the ideological spectrum.

For Jews familiar with the liturgy of the High Holy Days, or Abraham's debate with God over the fate of Sodom and Gemorrah, the Kohlberg-Gilligan argument is an old one. In Jewish tradition, God epitomizes both *din* and *rahamim*, justice and mercy. *Rahamim* comes from the root word *rehem*, or womb, thereby giving mercy a feminine voice. An approach to moral education in Jewish schools must include both justice and mercy. How does one teach for mercy, connectedness, or empathy? But a preliminary question: Can one teach for these qualities?

Some of the most interesting research on the subject of

empathy is being done by sociobiologists, or evolutionary psychologists as they are sometimes called. Edward O. Wilson (1998), who made his academic reputation studying the behavior of ants, is convinced that human activity, including moral behavior, can only be understood through biology. Is empathy natural, part of the make-up of all animal species? The question is not merely the clichéd nature-nurture teaser; the answers to it have profound educational implications. If empathy is in-born, then the task of the teacher (or parent) is straightforward: to elicit, through indirect, Socratic questioning, what is already there. However, if empathy is culturally determined and not genetic, then socialization (through the E's of Experience and Environment) must play a more dominant role. For example, learning empathy, like learning to say please and thank you or learning how to read and write, must be directly taught by parents and teachers.

Richard Wright (1994), a science writer, reviews the research of evolutionary biologists beginning with Darwin, cleverly applying it to moral concerns in Darwin's personal and professional life. Wright is unequivocal in concluding that there is nothing moral about animal empathy at all. Empathy is not natural. What we perceive as empathy or altruism is pure self-interest, what Dawkins (1989) called "the selfish gene." Through cold mathematical calculation designed to keep the genes of the species alive (called "kin selection" by sociobiologists), animals appear to be self-sacrificing. In fact, living things are programmed to be gene carriers whose sole biological purpose is to propagate their own DNA. Having arrived at the conclusion that empathy is not innate, Dawkins (1989) tells his readers that they cannot count on nature to produce children who instinctively know, love, and do the good. He concludes, "If there is a human moral to be drawn, it is that we must *teach* (italics his) our children altruism, for we cannot expect it to be a part of their biological nature." (p. 139)

Primatologist Frans de Waal (1996) takes the opposite view. De Waal studies chimpanzees and gorillas to learn about the roots of animal empathy. (He had the good fortune to publish his book while Americans were cooing over the exploits of Binti-Jua, the gorilla who carried a little boy to safety in Chicago's Brookfield Zoo.) Unlike Wright, Dawkins, et al., he is a believer that empathy is hard-wired in certain primates, and by extension, in humans as well. His writing is studded with examples of animal compassion. He describes a thirsty female chimpanzee struggling to get water and failing, only to be helped by a male who constructed a system to reach the water high above the animals' heads. He suggests that there is a high degree of correlation between a species' capacity for self-recognition in a mirror and displaying empathy toward its fellows. (Angier, May 9, 1995) In his view and that of cognitive psychologists as well, recognizing one's self in the other is a prerequisite for altruism.

Infants recognize themselves in mirrors during their second year of life, about the time that they display full-blown empathetic behavior. Both humans and animals display "mood contamination" (Angier, May 9, 1995): infants cry when they hear others wailing in a newborn nursery, like wolves and dogs who howl in unison. Psychologist Martin L. Hoffman has studied infant behavior and empathy for twenty years. He claims that empathy is the precursor to altruism. Hoffman (1977) has demonstrated that infants who cry in response to their nursery-mates are not doing so because they are frightened by the loud crying of their neighbors, but because they identify with them. (They do not cry in response to equally loud, artificially-induced noises.) We have all seen toddlers offer comfort to children and adults who are in pain, whether psychological or physical. Seeing the other person crying or wincing, the child will offer what works to console her: a favorite toy or blanket. To borrow the much-abused phrase of the nineties, she seems to feel another's pain. Hoffman contends that like cognition, empathy develops throughout childhood.

Using interviews with older children, Selman (Damon, 1983) concludes much as Piaget did a half-century before him, that morality is learned in friendships with peers. Role-taking, or perspective-sharing, is central to Selman's theory. Individuals who display this quality can project themselves into the situation of the other. But the ability to imagine another's pain does not necessarily result in altruism. One can appreciate someone's plight and still do nothing. Empathy researcher Eisenberg uses the example of highly empathetic nurses who avoid tending terminally ill patients because the experience is so painful for them. (Cited by Angier, May 5, 1995) Damon (1990) differentiates between empathy and sympathy; empathy is identifying with another's plight; sympathy is altruism, acting upon that feeling.

Eisenberg, Staub, and the Oliners claim that nurture, not nature, determines altruism. In their study of the altruistic behavior of those who helped Jews during the Holocaust, the Oliners (1988) identify a characteristic which they call "the extensive personality" —people who could apparently identify with others. These rescuers were more often than not raised by parents who were authoritative, while not authoritarian; had parents who extended themselves to others and thus witnessed acts of generosity to those outside the family circle; parents who reasoned with their children, and who, like the townspeople of Le Chambon who helped Jews survive during the Vichy regime in France, were often marginal themselves. The Oliners conclude:

> *In this context we suggest that the school—the social institution that alone commands attendance for a sustained length of time-can play an important role. Schools need to become institutions that not only prepare students for academic competence but also help them to acquire an extensive orientation to others. (p. 258)*

Ervin Staub (1993), a Holocaust survivor saved through the intervention of Raoul Wallenberg, has added to our knowledge of altruism by studying the behavior of bystanders. He learned that people who have undergone a course in CPR or life-saving are more likely to intervene to rescue those in difficulty than people who have not had this training. These findings indicate that schools, camps, and youth groups would do well to teach teenagers these skills. Even the youngest of children, as thousands of news stories will attest, can be taught to call 911. Feeling a certain degree of competence, young people will be more likely to translate compassion into action. (The voluminous literature on self-efficacy makes a convincing case for Staub's conclusions.) Citing the case of Oskar Schindler (Goleman, June 22, 1993) who took larger and larger risks for "his Jews," Staub also posits that one act of compassion is likely to lead to another, that truly as the rabbis taught, *mitzvah goreret mitzvah* (one good deed leads to another).

The name most likely to be associated with caring and education is Nel Noddings. A professor emerita of education at Stanford and professor at Columbia's Teachers College, her book A Challenge to Care in Schools (1992) is a handbook for designing a school curriculum around themes of care. In offering an alternative to the way schools are currently structured, Noddings (1995) expresses a feminist pedagogy. "(A curriculum based on caring) is an argument against the persistent undervaluing of skills, attitudes, and capacities traditionally associated with women." (p. 366) She also speaks the language of Martin Buber: "A caring relation is, in its most basic form, a connection or encounter between two human beings—a carer and a recipient of care, or cared-for." (Noddings, 1992, p. 15) Noddings (1992) suggests a curriculum that would work well in Jewish schools, or in Jewish camps. Imagine a set of concentric circles, with learners moving from the center toward the periphery. I've listed Noddings's domains of care with the equivalent Jewish value concepts below:

1. Caring for self (*B'tzelem Elohim*)
2. Caring in the inner circle (*Kibud av v'eim*)
3. Caring for strangers and distant others (*Gemilut hesed*)
4. Caring for animals, plants, and the earth (*Tza'ar ba'alei haim* and *bal tashhit*)
5. Caring for the human-made world (*Tikkun olam*)
6. Caring for ideas (*Talmud torah*).

The pedagogy is not only Deweyan, it meets the very Jewish

criteria set by the Maharal for good teaching: progress from the near to the far, from the concrete to the abstract. (Ingall, Summer 1994)

Like Noddings, Shlossman (1996) is convinced that Empathy can and must be taught. Her suggestions are based on her experience as a principal of a grades K-5 Jewish day school. Among them are:

1. Convening regularly scheduled school-wide assemblies in which she discusses an issue which might affect the group or she shares an act of compassion she has witnessed in the school;
2. Holding conversations about perspective-sharing (How does it feel to be the new kid in town? What can we do to make the new student more comfortable?);
3. Telling stories about caring; service projects;
4. Instituting cooperative learning opportunities;
5. Creating *mitzvah* trees highlighting acts of lovingkindness students witness within the school community and displaying them in public spaces;
6. Actively intervening in order to curtail meanness on the playground, in the halls, and in classrooms.

My former student, Beth, was very moved by a visit of the principal to the first-grade class in which she was doing her student teaching. One of the children had been in the hospital with a complicated illness. The principal folded his six-foot four frame into one of the student desks and told the intrigued youngsters that Yoni (a pseudonym) would be returning the following day, significantly weaker and thinner, and with tubes in his nose. He asked them how Yoni might feel upon his return. The students tossed out adjectives like nervous, strange, afraid, and embarrassed. Then the principal asked them to place themselves in Yoni's shoes. What might they like to have their classmates do for them tomorrow? Once again, they had no difficulty imagining an empathetic environment. They mentioned telling Yoni how much they missed him, sharing stories of their absences from school, hospitalizations, and reassuring Yoni that he didn't look funny at all. The following day my student reported that Yoni's return went without a hitch; she was amazed (and enormously moved) by how sensitive the children were. How can we teach Empathy? Through Exemplars like this compassionate principal and like the way we get to Carnegie Hall: practice, practice, practice.

HA-MA'ASEH

1. Have students call, visit, and collect assignments for their classmates who are ill or absent. Rotate the tasks so that students take the responsibility of helping people besides their friends. In either Hebrew or in English or both, create get-well cards for students who are ill.
2. In early childhood classes, add the job of Class Comforter to the roster of classroom tasks. The comforter's job is to soothe those who are upset. He can sit with a child who is upset and help calm him by playing together or reading until he is ready to rejoin the group.
3. Look for opportunities to take the perspective of others. Have students write a diary entry for one of Joseph's brothers; for a settler on Degania Aleph; for an Eastern European immigrant upon seeing the Statue of Liberty for the first time. These assignments can be done in Hebrew as well as in English.
4. Actively teach social skills. What does good listening look like? What does it sound like? What are put-ups? What are put-downs?
5. Pair older students with residents of a Jewish Home for the Aged in order to do a series of oral histories. Use this as an opportunity for the resident to reflect upon her life; for the student to learn about Jewish life in the earlier part of the 20th century. Have each party write a reflection on what she derived from the experience.
6. Instituting class buddies—pairing older students with younger ones—helps older students take the perspective of the other. Developing a relationship in class projects transcends to the playground. Teachers tell me of older buddies coming to the aid of their young ones—helping them tie shoes, climb playground equipment, and fend off classmates who tease them.
7. Teach and play some non-competitive games on the playground. For some students, recess is lonely and stressful.
8. Teach students conflict resolution skills which include imagining

how the other party feels.

9. While there is little available for school use on Salanter, the story "If Not Higher" by Y. L. Peretz is readily available in both Hebrew and English. Use it not only as a mood-setter before the High Holidays, but as a portrayal of Empathy.

10. Model the empathy and caring you expect of your students, not only to them, but to fellow faculty members as well. Students notice their teachers pinch-hitting in their colleagues' classes, sharing happy and sad moments in their personal lives, and wishing each other well for professional successes.

11. Some favorite classic Jewish sources on empathy:

a. The story about R. Akiva Eger (1761-1837) who had a dinner guest who unfortunately spilled wine on a sparkling white Sabbath tablecloth. Empathizing with his guest's profound embarrassment, Eger unobtrusively tipped over his own glass and apologized for the shakiness of the table (which, in actuality, was perfectly stable.)

b. A commentary on Exodus 17: 8-13: "Amalek came and fought with Israel at Rephidim. Moses said to Joshua, 'Pick some men for us, and go out and do battle with Amalek. Tomorrow I will station myself on the top of the hill, with the rod of God in my hand.' Joshua did as Moses told him and fought with Amalek, while Moses, Aaron, and Hur went up to the top of the hill. Then, whenever Moses held up his hand, Israel prevailed; but whenever he let down his hand, Amalek prevailed. But Moses's hands grew heavy; so they took a stone on each side, supported his hands; thus his hands remained steady until the sun set. And Joshua overwhelmed the people of Amalek with the sword."

"Rather a man should share in the distress of the community, for so we find that Moses, our teacher, shared in the distress of the community, as it is said: 'But Moses's hands were heavy, and they took a stone, and put it under him, and he sat thereon. Did not then Moses have a bolster or a cushion to sit on? This is then what Moses meant to convey: 'As Israel is in distress, I too will share with them. He who shares in the distress of the community will merit to behold its consolation.' (Ta'anit 11a)

c. I thank Rabbi Edward Bernstein who called this text from Mekhilta Masekhta D'Pisha, 14 to my attention: *Even the selfsame day it came to pass, that all the hosts of the Lord went out from the land of Egypt*. The hosts of the Lord are the ministering angels. And so you find that whenever Israel is enslaved, the Shekhina, as it were, is enslaved with them. So far I know only that He shares in the affliction of the community. How about the affliction of the individual? Scripture says: 'He shall call upon Me, and I will answer him; I will be with him in trouble' [Ps. 91:15]

AFTERWORD

Susan Ohanian (1992) describes teachers as being hungry for "stir-and-serve" recipes. Sad to say, in the realm of moral education, there are no simple formulas. Each school culture is so idiosyncratic that it is complete *hutzpah* to prescribe unilaterally. Believing as I do in the social construction of knowledge, I am convinced that each school has to create an approach to moral education that works for its milieu. That process of galvanizing a school community can be exhausting and frustrating, but as Aron, Lee, and Rossel (1995) chronicle in their volume on school change, also energizing and rewarding. Convening the forum can afford administrators, faculty, and parents opportunities for the fundamental but rarely held conversations about what it means to be a good person and good Jew and how to nurture that goodness.

A corollary of the "no recipes" dictum is that there are no shortcuts, no monistic solutions. Any program the school creates (in tandem with all the stakeholders) has to be multi-dimensional, organic, and far-reaching. The occasional school assembly, the 9:00-9:50 a.m. class in moral education, and the annual *Tikkun Olam* project are not effective. A thoughtful program in moral education must permeate every aspect of school life, every classroom, and every interaction with parents. Moral education must be taught across the curriculum; knowing the good, loving the good, and doing the good must be found in classrooms, playing fields, cafeterias, and the principal's office.

Although I am a multiplist regarding solutions to complicated social issues, I have to admit to one absolutist principle: Any program in moral education that does not include the realms of thought, feeling, and action is doomed. I am not dismayed by the Hartshorne and May (1928) studies which proclaimed moral education efforts in schools to be failures. I firmly believe that schools can make a difference; there is a huge literature which makes that point far more effectively than I can. (Lightfoot, 1983;

Hill et al., 1990; Rutter et al., 1979) What Hartshorne and May really proved was that moral education **poorly** done doesn't make a difference.

To effect such a wide-reaching program of moral education, the administrator must convince her teachers that moral education is not an overlay or an insert to their curricula. It is not an add-on, yet another serving on an already heaped plate. What the teachers will be asked to do is to reorganize around moral frameworks, to find teachable moments in their pre-existing curricula, to be thoughtful about their class environment (physical and psychological), and be conscious of the enormous power they wield as moral exemplars. Good teachers do a great deal of this by instinct; what I am asking is that they do this self-consciously, reflectively, and as a community.

All right. I'll confess to a second absolutist principle. Any approach to moral education must include a combination of "outside-in" and "inside-out" pedagogy. We have to struggle with the tension between authenticity and relevance—teaching the tradition as stewards of cultural literacy while helping students to connect to it as moderns, living in a culture of choice. Note: I do not say that we should help them to resolve that tension. As educators we are obligated to first introduce them to that tension, then help them understand that the challenge of modernity is to live with that tension. Rooted as they are in American life, our students will not be moved by an approach of "Here are the rules. Follow them" or the school equivalent of "Three strikes and you're out." On the other hand, a model which is slavishly wedded to *pareve* universalism or trivial self-esteem-building is unworthy of a Jewish educational institution. What I've tried to suggest in this book is an approach which honors canon but allows for the construction of personal meaning, which blends both the normative and the intuitive, which synthesizes transmission and transformation. I've sketched out the parameters; the guts of the program are for the school to create. Each school will attach different valences to the "outside-in" and the "inside-out," just as they will to the categories of knowing the good, loving the good, and doing the good.

Are there only eight elements in this philosophy? Audiences repeatedly hurl the same question at Howard Gardner: How does he know that there are only seven intelligences in his theory of multiple intelligences? (In fact, he added an eighth, the naturalistic intelligence, this past year.) Gardner responds that as far as he is concerned there could be twenty or more. What matters is that teachers have traditionally valued a limited range of talents. For students to succeed in life, their learning will have to become more diverse, more personalized, and more social. Similarly, I hold no brief for eight, not seven or nine, strands of moral education. What matters is the diversity of approaches, the organicity of the program, the weaving of the normative and the intuitive, and the tapping into the resources of thought, action, and feeling.

If we don't turn our attention into creating schools which are greenhouses to nurture children's moral development, we have betrayed our trust to the community. We disappoint the parents who send their children to us as well. In a recent article, David Ackerman (1997) examines parent orientation programs in four schools. (They were day schools, but I would imagine his findings could relate to synagogue schools, JCC programs, and camps as well.) He notes that these schools did not market themselves as places which nurture values, or to borrow the felicitous phrase used by Baden-Powell to describe the Boy Scouts (Rosenthal, 1986), "character factories," despite parents' interest in this arena. We ignore this domain, as difficult as it may be, at our peril. To give short shrift to moral education in our schools is to dishonor our past and to deny us a future.

REFERENCES

Abohav, Y. ([14th c.] 1984). Menoras Hamaor: Parents and children. Lakewood, NJ: Creative Institutional Services.

Abrahams, I. (Ed.) (1926). Hebrew ethical wills. Philadelphia: Jewish Publication Society of America.

Abramson, R. (1990, March). Kedushah: One focus in the vision of our day schools. The Melton Journal, (23), 32 ff.

Ackerman, D. (1997, March). Marketing Jewish education. Journal of Jewish Education, 63(1 & 2), 70-76.

Ahad Ha-'am (1912). Selected essays by Ahad Ha-'am. L. Simon, (Trans.) . Philadelphia: Jewish Publication Society of America.

Althusser, L. (1976). Essays in self-criticism. London: New Left Books.

Angier, N. (1995, May 9). Scientists mull role of empathy in man and beast. The New York Times, p. 1; 6.

Aristotle (1985). Nicomachaean ethics. Indianapolis: Hackett Publishing Co.

Aron, I., Lee, S., & Rossel, S. (Eds.) (1995). A congregation of leaders: Transforming the synagogue into a learning community. New York: UAHC Press.

Bachya ben Joseph ibn Paquda ([11th c .]1941). Duties of the heart. NewYork: Bloch Publishing Co.

Bayme, S. A. (1996, March). Agenda: Jewish education, (7), 27-29.

Bellah, R. N., Madsen, R., Sullivan, W. M., Swidler, A., & Tipton, S. M. (1985). Habits of the heart: Individualism and commitment in American life. New York: Harper & Row.

Bennett, W. J. (1993). The book of virtues: A treasury of great moral stories. New York: Simon & Schuster.

Berger, P. (1990). The sacred canopy: Elements of a sociological theory of religion. New York: Anchor Books.

Berger, P. L., & Luckmann, T. (1966). The social construction of reality: A treatise in the sociology of knowledge. New York: Doubleday.

Bialik, H. N. , & Ravnitzky, Y. H. (1992). The book of legends (*Sefer ha-aggadah*). (Trans. William G. Braude.) New York: Schocken Books.

Blaisdell, A. F., & Ball, F. K. (1915). Heroic deeds of American sailors. Boston: Little, Brown & Co.

Bruner, J. (1986). Actual minds, possible worlds. Cambridge, MA: Harvard University Press.

Buber, M. (1965). Between man and man. New York: Macmillan.

Bullis, H. E., & O'Malley, E. E. (1952). Human relations in the classroom course. Wilmington, DE: Delaware State Society for Mental Hygiene.

Casey, M. B., & Tucker, E. C. (October 1994). Problem-centered classrooms: Creating lifelong learners. Phi Delta Kappan 76 (2), 139-143.

Chazan, B. (1980). Jewish education and moral development. In B. Munsey, (Ed.) Moral education: The debate in philosophy, psychology, religion, and education. Birmingham, AL: Religious Education Press, pp. 298-325.

Cohen, B. (1984). The teaching of deliberation in the Jewish school. In M. Rosenak, (Ed.) Studies in Jewish Education, vol. 2. Jerusalem: Magnes Press, the Hebrew University.

Cohen, B. (1985). The secret grove. New York: Union of American Hebrew Congregations.

Coles, R. (1993). The call of service: A witness to idealism. Boston: Houghton Mifflin Co.

Cooper, A. (March, 1996). Parental responsibility for the Jewish upbringing of small children: Some traditional sources. CCAR Journal: A Reform Jewish Quarterly, 43(2), 19-30.

Cremin, L. A. (1977). Traditions of American education. New York: Basic Books.

Damon, W. (1995). Greater expectations. New York: The Free Press.

Damon, W. (1990). The moral child. New York: The Free Press.Day, J. M. (1991).

Dawkins, R. (1989) The selfish gene. New York: Oxford University Press.

Day, J. M. The moral audience: On the narrative mediation of moral "judgment" and moral "action". In M. B. Tappan & M. J. Packer (Eds.), Narrative and storytelling: Implications for understanding moral development (New Directions for Child Development) Vol. 54, San Francisco: Jossey-Bass, Inc., pp. 27-42.

Delattre, E. J. (1992, September). Teaching integrity: The boundaries of moral education. Letters from Santa Fe.

de Waal, F. (1996). Good natured: The origins of right and wrong in humans and other animals. Cambridge, MA: Harvard University Press.

Dorff, E. N. ,& Newman, L. E. (1995). Contemporary Jewish ethics and morality: A reader. New York: Oxford University Press.

Dorff, E. N. (1989). Mitzvah means commandment. New York: United Synagogue of America: Department of Youth Activities.

Dresner, S. H. (1982) The Jewish dietary laws: Their meaning for our time. New York: Rabbinical Assembly; United Synagogue Commission on Jewish Education.

Durkheim, E. (1956). Education and sociology. New York: The Free Press.

REFERENCES

Durkheim, E. (1973). Moral education: A study in the theory and application of the sociology of education. New York: The Free Press.

Efron, S. (1996, December). Jewish moral education and character education: A comparison. Journal of Jewish Education, 62(1), 4-13.

Eisner, E. W. (1985). The educational imagination: On the design and evaluation of school programs. New York: Macmillan Publishing Company.

Elkind, D. (1988). The hurried child: Growing up too fast too soon. Reading, MA: Addison-Wesley.

Elkins, D. P. (1977). Clarifying Jewish values: A handbook of value clarification strategies for group leaders, educators, rabbis, teachers, center workers and counselors. Princeton, NJ: Growth Associates.

Etkes, I. (1993). Rabbi Israel Salanter and the mussar movement. Philadelphia: Jewish Publication Society .

Faludi, S. (1991). Backlash: The undeclared war against American women. New York: Crown.

Fishman, S. B. (1996). Negotiating both sides of the hyphen: Coalescence, compartmentalization, and American-Jewish values. Cincinnati: University of Cincinnati Judaic Studies Program.

Fowler, J. W. (1981). Stages of faith: The psychology of human development and the quest for meaning. New York: HarperCollins.

Galbraith, R. E., & Jones, T. M. (1976). Moral reasoning: A teaching handbook for adapting Kohlberg to the classroom. n. p.: Greenhaven Press.

Gardner, H. (1983). Frames of mind. New York: Basic Books.

Gardner, H. (1991). The unschooled mind: How children think and how schools should teach. New York: Basic Books.

Gaster, M. (Ed.) (1981). *Ma'aseh* book. Philadelphia: Jewish Publication Society of America.

Gilligan, C. (1982). In a different voice: Psychological theory and women's development. Cambridge, MA: Harvard University Press.

The Giraffe Project (1991). Giraffes in schools: The standing tall program. Langley, WA: The Giraffe Project.

Glenn, M. G. (1953). Israel Salanter: Religious-ethical thinker. New York: Bloch.

Goffman, E. (1961). Asylums: Essays on the social situation of mental patients and other inmates. Garden City, NY: Anchor Books.

Goldberg, H. (1972). Musar anthology. Boston: Jewish Student Projects and Jewish Association for College Youth.

Goldhagen, D. J. (1996). Hitler's willing executioners: Ordinary Germans and the

Holocaust. New York: Alfred A. Knopf.

Goleman, D. (1995). Emotional intelligence. New York: Bantam Books.

Goleman, D. (1993, June 22). Studying the pivotal role of bystanders. The New York Times, p. 1; 6.

Greene, M. (1985). The role of education in democracy. Educational Horizons, (63), 3-9.

Greer, C., & Kohl, H. (1995). A call to character. New York: HarperCollins.

Grishaver, J. L., & Huppin, B. (1983). *Tzedakah, gemilut chasadim* and *ahavah*: A manual for world repair Denver, CO: Alternatives in Religious Education.

Hallie, P. (1985). Lest innocent blood be shed: The story of the village of Le Chambon and how goodness happened there. New York: Harper & Row.

Halper, B. (Ed.). (1921). Post-biblical literature: An anthology. Philadelphia: Jewish Publication Society of America.

Hartshorne, H., & May, M. A. (1928). Studies in the nature of character: Vol. 1. Studies in deceit. New York: Macmillan.

Havighurst, R., & Taba, H. (1949). Adolescent character and personality. New York: John Wiley & Sons.

Heinemann, I. (1953). *Ta'ame ha-mitzvot besifrut Yisrael*. Jerusalem: Hamador ha-dati, ha mahlaka l'inyene ha-noar v'hehalutz shel hahalat ha-Histadrut.

Henry, M. E. (1993). School cultures: Universes of meaning in private schools. Norwood, NJ: Ablex Publishing Corp.

Hertz, J. H. (Ed.) (1956) The Pentateuch and haftorahs./ London: Soncino Press.

Heschel, A. J. (1956). God in search of man: A philosophy of Judaism. Philadelphia: Jewish Publication Society of America.

Hill, P. T., Foster, G. E., & Gendler, T. (1990). High schools with character. Santa Monica, CA: RAND.

Hoffman, M. (1976). Empathy, role-taking, guilt, and development of altruistic motives. In T. Lickona (Ed.), Moral development and behavior. New York: Holt, Rinehart, and Winston.

Hoffman, M. L. (1977). Moral internalization: Current theory and research. In L. Berkowitz (Ed.), Advances in experimental social psychology. Vol. 10. New York: Academic Press.

Huffman, H. A. (1994). Developing a character education program: One school district's experience. Alexandria, VA: ASCD.

Ibn Gabirol. S. ([11th c.]1925). The wisdom of Ibn Gabirol. New York: Bloch Publishing Co.

Ingall, C. K. (1994). Cooperative or collaborative learning. In A. F. Marcus & R.

A. Zwerin, (Eds.) The New Jewish Teachers Handbook, Denver, CO: A.R.E., pp. 127-135.

Ingall, C. K. (1997). Maps. metaphors, and mirrors: Moral education in middle schools. Greenwich, CT: Ablex Publishing Co.

Ingall, C. K. (Spring 1998). The Nahshon School: Portrait of a caring community. Religious Education 93(2), 227-240.

Ingall, C. K. (Summer 1994). Reform and redemption: The Maharal of Prague and John Amos Comenius. Religious Education, 89(3), 358-375.

Israel, R. J. (1995). Jewish tradition and political action. In E. N. Dorff & L. E. Newman,(Eds.) Contemporary Jewish ethics and morality: A reader, New York: Oxford University Press, pp. 118-128.

Jensen, E. (1998). Teaching with the brain in mind. Alexandria, VA: Association for Supervision & Curriculum Development.

Johnson, M. (1993). Moral imagination: Implications of cognitive science for ethics. Chicago: University of Chicago Press.

Kadushin, M. (1952). The rabbinic mind. New York: Jewish Theological Seminary of America.

Kagan, J. (1984). The nature of the child. New York: Basic Books.

Kahne, J., & Westheimer, J. (1996, May). In the service of what? The politics of service learning. Phi Delta Kappan, 77(9), 593-99.

Kierkegaard, S. (1940). The present age. London: Oxford University Press.

Kirschenbaum, H. (1995). 100 ways to enhance values and morality in schools and youth settings. Needham Heights, MA: Allyn & Bacon.

Kirschner, R. (Ed. & Trans.) (1985). Rabbinic responsa of the Holocaust era. New York: Schocken Books.

Kobler, F. (Ed.). (1978). Letters of Jews through the ages. Vol. I. Philadelphia: Jewish Publication Society.

Kohlberg, L. (1969). Stage and sequence: The cognitive-developmental approach to socialization. In D. Goslin (Ed.), Handbook of socialization theory and research. New York: Rand McNally, pp. 347-480.

Kohn, A. (February, 1997). How not to teach values: A critical look at character education. Phi Delta Kappan, 78(6), 428-439.

Lampert, M. (1988). The teacher's role in reinventing the meaning of mathematical knowing in the classroom. Research series no. 186. East Lansing, MI: The Institute for Research on Teaching, College of Education, Michigan State University.

Lasch, C. (1978). The culture of narcissism: American life in an age of diminishing expectations. New York: W. W. Norton.

Levinas, E. (1994). Nine talmudic readings. Bloomington, IN: University of Indiana Press.

Lickona, T. (1992). Educating for character: How our schools can teach respect and responsibility. New York: Bantam.

Liebman, C. S. (1975). The religion of American Jews. In J. Neusner, (Ed.) Understanding American Judaism Vol. I, New York: Ktav.

Lightfoot, S. L. (1983). The good high school: Portraits of character and culture. New York: Basic Books, Inc.

Lockwood, A. T. (1997). Conversations with educational leaders: Contemporary viewpoints on education in America. Albany: State University of New York Press.

Luzzatto, M. H. ([1740]1948). *Mesillat yesharim*, Philadelphia: Jewish Publication Society.

MacIntyre, A. (1984). After virtue. Notre Dame, IN: University of Notre Dame Press.

Maimonides ([12th c.]1967). *Mishneh Torah (Yad Hazakah)*. New York: Hebrew Publishing Company.

Marchant, D. (1998). *Sefer Chofetz Chaim* with the commentary *Yad Dovid*, Vol. 1. Jerusalem: Feldheim Publishers.

(1837). McGuffey's third eclectic reader. Rev. edition. New York: American Book Company.

Mosier, R. D. (1965). Making the American mind: Social and moral ideas in the McGuffey Readers. New York: Russell and Russell, Inc.

Neusner, J. (Trans.). (1984). Torah from our sages: Pirke Avot. Chappaqua, NY: Rossel Books.

Noddings, N. (1992). The challenge to care in schools: An alternative approach to education. New York: Teachers College Press.

Noddings, N. (1995, January). A morally defensible mission for schools in the 21st century. Phi Delta Kappan, 76(5), 365-368.

Ohanian, S. (1992). On stir-and-serve recipes for teaching. In K. Ryan & J. M. Cooper (Eds.) Kaleidoscope: Readings in Education. 6th Ed. Boston: Houghton Mifflin Company, 48-53.

Oliner, S. P., & Oliner, P. M. (1988). The altruistic personality: Rescuers of Jews in Nazi Europe. New York: The Free Press.

Parker, W. C. (1997, February). The art of deliberation. Educational Leadership, 54(5), 18-21.

Peters, R. S. (1981). Moral development and moral education. London: George

Allen and Unwin.

Pickering, W. (1984). Durkheim's sociology of religion: Themes and theories. London: Routledge and Kegan Paul.

Power, C. (1988, October). The just community approach to moral education. The Journal of Moral Education, 17(3), 195-208.

Price, Ron. (1995) Media and Torah values. Teaneck, NJ: Union of Traditional Judaism.

Purpel, D., & Ryan, K. (Eds.). (1976). Moral education: It comes with the territory. Berkeley, CA: McCutchan Publishing Corp.

Raths, L., Harmin, M., & Simon, S. (1966). Values and teaching: Working with values in the classroom. Columbus, OH: Charles E. Merrill Publishing Co.

Riemer, J. &. Stampfer, N. (1983). Ethical wills: A modern Jewish treasury. New York: Schocken Books.

Rosenak, M. (1983). Jewish religious education and indoctrination. In B. Chazan, (Ed.)Studies in Jewish education Vol. Vol. I, Jerusalem: The Magnes Press, pp. 117-138.

Rosenak, M. (1995). Roads to the palace: Jewish texts and teaching. Providence, RI: Berghahn Books.

Rosenak, M. (1986). Teaching Jewish values: A conceptual guide. Jerusalem: The Melton Center for Jewish Education in the Diaspora of the Hebrew University of Jerusalem.

Rosenheck, R. (1998). Portrait of Allison Kahn: Student, scholar, and teacher of talmud. Unpublished manuscript.

Rosenthal, M. (1986). The character factory: Baden-Powell's boy scouts and the imperatives of empire. New York: Pantheon.

Rosenzweig, F. (1955). On Jewish learning. New York: Schocken Books.

Rothstein, E. (1997, April 7). Cursive, foiled again. New York Times, p. 1, 7.

Rutter, M., Maughan, B., Mortimore, P., & Ouston, J., with Smith, A. (1979). Fifteen thousand hours: Secondary schools and their effects on children. Cambridge: Harvard University Press.

Ryan, K. (1988). The new moral education. In K. Ryan & J. Cooper (Eds.), Kaleidoscope: Readings in education (5th ed.), (pp. 286-293). Boston: Houghton Mifflin.

Sarbin, T. R. (Ed.) (1986). Narrative psychology: The storied nature of human conduct. New York: Praeger.

Scheffler, I. (1995). Teachers of my youth: An American Jewish experience. Boston: Kluwer Academic Publishers.

Schimmel, S. (1983). Ethical dimensions of traditional Jewish education. In B.

Chazan, (Ed.) Studies in Jewish Education, Vol. I, (pp. pp. 91-111). Jerusalem: The Magnes Press.

Schwartz, B. L. (1996). Jewish heroes, Jewish values: Living mitzvot in today's world. West Orange, NJ: Behrman House.

Schwartz, E. (1983). Moral development: A practical guide for Jewish teachers. Denver, CO: Alternatives in Religious Education.

Sergiovanni, T. J. (1992). Moral leadership: Getting to the heart of school improvement. San Francisco: Jossey-Bass Publishers.

Shlossman, R. (1996, March). Can you teach empathy? Tikkun, 11(2), 20-22.

(1985). Siddur Sim Shalom: A prayerbook for Shabbat, festivals, and weekdays. (Ed. & Trans. by Jules Harlow) New York: The Rabbinical Assembly.

Siegel, D. (1993). Tell me a mitzvah: Little and big ways to repair the world. Rockville, MD: Karben Copies, Inc.

Simon, S. B., Howe, L., & Kirschenbaum, H. (1972). Values clarification: A handbook of practical strategies for teachers and students. New York: Hart.

Simon, S. B., & Olds, S. W. (1977). Helping your child learn right from wrong: A guide to values clarification. New York: McGraw Hill.

Skinner, B. F. (1962). Walden two. New York: The MacMillan Company.

Slavson, S. (1948). Creative group education. New York: Association Press.

Sommers, C. H. (1984). Ethics without virtue: Moral education in America. American Scholar, 53(3), 381-389.

Staub, E. (Summer, 1993). The psychology of bystanders, perpetrators, and heroic helpers. International Journal of Intercultural Relations, 17(3), 315-341.

Tishman, S., & Perkins, D. (January, 1997). The language of thinking. Phi Delta Kappan, 78(5), 368-374.

(1981). The Torah: A modern commentary. Commentaries by W. Gunther Plaut. New York: Union of American Hebrew Congregations.

Twersky, I. (Ed.). (1972). A Maimonides reader. New York: Behrman House.

Walker, L. J. (June 1984) Sex differences in the development of moral reasoning: A critical review. Child Development 55(3), 677-691.

Wechter, J. D. (1981). Adolescent ego ideal development and its relationship to psychosexual level. Unpublished Doctoral dissertation, Boston University Graduate School of Education, Boston.

Weiss, B. J. (Ed.) (1982). American education and the European immigrant: 1840-1940. Urbana, IL: University of Illinois Press.

Wilson, E. O. (1998). Consilience: The unity of knowledge. New York: Knopf.

References

Wolpe, D. J. (1990). The healer of shattered hearts: A Jewish view of God. New York: H. Holt.

Woodward, K. L. (1990). Making saints: How the Catholic Church determines who becomes a saint, who doesn't, and why. New York: A Touchstone Book.

Wright, R. (1994). The moral animal: Why we are the way we are. The new science of evolutionary psychology. New York: Pantheon Books.

Wuthnow, R. (1994). Producing the sacred: An essay on public religion. Urbana: University of Illinois Press.

Wynne, E. (1986). The great tradition in education: Transmitting moral values. Educational Leadership, 43(1), 4-9.

Yulish, S. (1980). The search for civic religion: History of the character education movement in America: 1890-1935. Washington, DC: University Press of America.

INDEX

NOTE: Page numbers followed by "n" refer to footnotes; page numbers followed by "t" refer to tables.

Index

Index to Non-Biblical Sources

רבי אלעזר בן שמוע אומר: יהי כבוד תלמידך חביב עליך כשלך, וכבוד חברך כמורא רבך, ומורא רבך כמורא שמים. פרקי אבות ד: טו (p. 8)

והמתכבד בקלון חברו אין לו חלק לעולם הבא [ירושלמי חגיגה ב, הלכה א]. רמב״ם, משנה תורה דעות ו:ג (p. 8)

רבי טרפון אומר: היום קצר, והמלאכה מְרֻבָּה, והפועלים עצלים, והשכר הרבה, ובעל הבית דוחק.
הוא היה אומר: לא עליך המלאכה לגמור, ולא אתה בן-חורין לִבָּטֵל ממנה. פרקי אבות ב:כ-כא (p. 10)

משה קִבֵּל תורה מסיני ומסרה ליהושע, ויהושע לזקנים, וזקנים לנביאים. ונביאים מסרוּהָ לאנשי כנסת הגדולה. הם אמרו שלושה דברים: הוו מתונים בדין. והעמידו תלמידים הרבה. ועשו סְיָג לתורה. פרקי אבות א:א (p. 30)

ללכת בכל-דרכיו. אֵילוּ דרכי הקדוש ברוך הוא, שנאמר: יהוה יהוה אל רחום וחנון ארך אַפַּיִם ורב חסד ואמת, נוצר חסד לאלפים נושא עָוֺן ופשע וחטאה ונקה.... מה המקום נקרא רחום וחנון, אף אתה הֱוֵי רחום וחנון.... מה הקדוש ברוך הוא נקרא צדיק, שנאמר, צדיק יהוה בכל-דרכיו, אף אתה הוי צדיק. הקדוש ברוך הוא נקרא חסיד, שנאמר, וחסיד בכל-מעשיו, אף אתה הוי חסיד. ספרי - עקב (p. 32)

ולא יקפֵּץ ידו ביותר ולא יפזר ממונו, אלא נותן צדקה כפי מִסַּת ידו וּמַלְוֶה כראוי למי שצריך. ולא יהא מהולל ושוחק ולא עצב ואונן, אלא שמח כל ימיו בנחת, בסבר פנים יפות. וכן שאר דֵעוֹתָיו. ודרך זו היא דרך החכמים. כל אדם שדֵעוֹתָיו דעות בינוניות, מְמֻצָּעוֹת, נקרא חכם. רמב״ם, משנה תורה דעות א:ד (pp. 32-33)

האדם חָפשי בדמיונו, ואסור במושכלו. דמיונו מוליכו שובב בדרך לב רצונו, בל יחת מהעתיד הודאי, עת יפקוד ה׳ על כל מפעליו, ובשפטים קשים יוסר, בל ילכד זר בגללו, הוא לבדו ישא פרי חטאו, אחד הוא, העושה הָעֲבֵרָה והנענש. מרה היא, בל יאמר האדם זה חלי ואשאנו. ר׳ ישראל סלנטר, אגרת המוסר (p. 33)

אלו דברים שאין להם שִׁעוּר: הפאה והבִּכּוּרים והראיון וגמילות חסדים ותלמוד תורה. משנה פאה א:א (p. 34)

אלו דברים שאדם אוכל פרותיהם בעולם הזה והקרן קַיֶּמֶת לו לעולם הבא, ואלו הן: כִּבּוּד אב ואם, וגמילות חסדים, והשכמת בית המדרש שחרית וערבית, והכנסת אורחים, ובקור חולים, והכנסת כלה, וּלְוָיַת המת, וְעִיּוּן תפלה, והבאת שלום בין אדם לחברו ובין איש לאשתו, ותלמוד תורה כנגד כֻּלָּם. שבת קכז:א (p. 34)

תנו רבנן: לעולם יהא אדם רך כקנה ואל יהא קשה כארז. מעשה שבא רבי אלעזר ברבי שמעון ממגדל גדור מבית רבו, והיה רכוב על חמור וּמְטַיֵּל על שפת נהר. ושמח שמחה גדולה, והיתה דעתו גסה עליו מפני שלמד תורה הרבה. נזדמן לו אדם אחד שהיה מכוער ביותר. אמר לו שלום עליך רבי, ולא החזיר לו. אמר לו ריקה כמה מכוער אותו האיש שמא כל בני עירך מכוערין כמותך. אמר לו איני יודע אלא לך ואמור לאומן שעשאני כמה מכוער כלי זה שעשית. כיון שידע בעצמו שחטא ירד מן החמור ונשתטח לפניו ואמר לו, נעניתי לך מחול לי. אמר לו איני מוחל לך עד שתלך לאומן שעשאני ואמור לו כמה מכוער כלי זה שעשית. היה מטייל אחריו עד שהגיע לעירו. יצאו בני עירו לקראתו והיו אומרים לו שלום עליך רבי רבי מורי מורי. אמר להם למי אתם קורין רבי רבי. אמרו לו לזה שמטייל אחריך. אמר להם אם זה רבי אל ירבו כמותו בישראל. אמרו לו מפני מה? אמר להם, כך וכך עשה לי. אמרו לו אע״פ כן מחול לו שאדם גדול בתורה הוא. אמר להם בשבילכם הריני מוחל לו ובלבד שלא יהא רגיל לעשות כן. מיד נכנס רבי אלעזר בן רבי שמעון ודרש, לעולם יהא אדם רך כקנה ואל יהא קשה כארז. ולפיכך זכה קנה ליטול הימנה קולמוס לכתוב בו ספר תורה תפילין ומזוזות. <u>**תענית**</u> כ:א-ב (p. 35)

דבר אחר ׳גֹּמֵל נפשו איש חסד׳ זה הלל הזקן שבשעה שהיה נפטר מתלמידיו היה מהלך והולך עִמָּם אמרו לו תלמידיו רבי להיכן אתה הולך, אמר להם לִגְמֹל חסד עם הדין אכסניא בגו ביתא. אמרו לו כל יום אית לך אכסניא. אמר להם והדין נפשא עלובתא לאו אכסניא הוא בגו גופא יומא דין היא הכא למחר לית היא הכא. <u>**ויקרא רבא**</u> לג:ג (p. 36)

״הנך נמי בני עלמא דאתי נינהו״. אזל לגבייהו אמר להו: ״מאי עובדייכו?״ אמרו ליה: ״אינשי בדוחי אנן, מבדחינן עציבי. אי נמי, כי חזינן בי תרי דאית להו תיגרא בהדייהו, טרחינן ועבדינן להו שלמא״. <u>**תענית**</u> כב:א (p. 36)

רבן יוחנן בן זכאי קִבֵּל מהלל ומשמאי. הוא היה אומר: אם למדת תורה הרבה, אל תחזיק טובה לעצמך, כי לכך נוצרת.

חמישה תלמידים היו לו לרבן יוחנן בן זכאי, ואלו הן: רבי אליעזר בן הֻרְקְנוֹס, רבי יהושע בן חנניא, רבי יוסי הכהן, רבי שמעון בן נתנאל, ורבי אלעזר בן ערך. <u>**פרקי אבות**</u> ב:ט-י (p. 39)

יהי רצון מלפניך יהוה אלהי ואלהי אבותי, שתצילני היום ובכל-יום מעזי פנים ומעזות פנים, מאדם רע ומחבר רע, ומשכן רע ומפגע רע ומשטן המשחית, מדין קשה ומבעל דין קשה, בין שהוא בן-ברית ובין שאינו בן-ברית. <u>**סידור שים שלום**</u> ע׳ יב (p. 39)

אמר רבי יוסי בן קסמא: פעם אחת הייתי מהלך בדרך, ופגע בי אדם אחד ונתן לי שלום, והחזרתי לו שלום. אמר לי: רבי, מאיזה מקום אתה.

ואמר רבי חייא בר אבא אמר ר׳ יוחנן כל תלמיד חכם שנמצא רבב על בגדו חייב מיתה שנאמר כל משנאי אהבו מות אל תקרי משנאי אלא משניאי רבניא אמר רבד איתמר ולא פליגי הא בגלימא הא בלבושא. **שבת** קיד:א (pp. 117-118)

אלא: יצער אדם עם הצבור. שכן מצינו במשה רבינו שציער עצמו עם הצבור, שנאמר ״וידי משה כבדים ויקחו אבן וישימו תחתיו וישב עליה״. וכי לא היו לו למשה כר אחד או כסת אחת לישן עליה? אלא כך אמר משה: הואיל וישראל שרויין בצער - אף אני אהיה עמהם בצער, וכל המצער עצמו עם הצבור - זוכה ורואה בנחמת הצבור. **תענית** יא:א (p. 133)

ויהי בעצם היום הזה יצאו כל צבאות יי אלו מלאכי השרת וכן אתה מוצא כל זמן שישראל משועבדין כביכול שכינה משועבדת עמהן שנ׳ ויראו את אלהי ישראל ותחת רגליו כמעשה לבנת הספיר (שמות כד י). וכשנגאלו מה הוא אומר וכעצם השמים לטוהר ונאמר בכל צרתם לו צר (ישעיה סג ט). אין לי אלא צרת ציבור צרת יחיד מנין ת״ל יקראני ואענהו עמו אנכי בצרה (תלים מא טו). **מכילתא** מסכת דפסחא יד (p. 134)

www.ingramcontent.com/pod-product-compliance
Ingram Content Group UK Ltd.
Pitfield, Milton Keynes, MK11 3LW, UK
UKHW041831290726
14061UKWH00004BA/191/J